BOOKS BY JASON WEBSTER

Duende: A Journey in Search of Flamenco

Andalus: Unlocking the Secrets of Moorish Spain

¡Guerra!: Living in the Shadows of the Spanish Civil War

Sacred Sierra: A Year on a Spanish Mountain

The Spy with 29 Names: The Story of the Second World War's Most Audacious Double Agent

Violencia: A New History of Spain

THE MAX CÁMARA CRIME NOVELS

Or the Bull Kills You

A Death in Valencia

The Anarchist Detective

Blood Med

A Body in Barcelona

Fatal Sunset

MOSAICS OF SPAIN SERIES

Volume I: The World of Max Cámara

THE ART OF FLAMENCO

MOSAICS OF SPAIN VOLUME II

JASON WEBSTER

CORSARIO

CORSARIO

www.corsariobooks.com
info@corsariobooks.com

First published by Corsario, 2020

THE ART OF FLAMENCO
MOSAICS OF SPAIN VOLUME II

Copyright © Jason Webster

www.jasonwebster.net

The right of Jason Webster to be identified
as the owner of this work has been asserted by them in accordance
with the Copyright, Designs and Patents Act 1988.

ISBN: 978-1-913955-02-1

All rights reserved
Copyright throughout the world

No part of this publication may be reproduced or transmitted in any form or by any means, electronic, mechanical or photographic, by recording or any information storage or retrieval system or method now known or to be invented or adapted, without prior permission obtained in writing from the publisher, Corsario Books, except by a reviewer quoting brief passages in a review written for inclusion in a journal, magazine, newspaper, blog or broadcast.

FOR

My brother Chris

'What is duende*? I think it's a moment, a feeling, an instant when you are flowing into that space which is "above". It's something mystical.*

And I think it not only exists in flamenco. Probably all artists can feel it when they are flowing… It's so difficult; I can't explain.

'It's like you are in an expression. You are not "out of yourself ", because you are in yourself, but you are in a different place, you are flowing. And possibly painters when they know what they are doing, and time is passing, they are having that experience of duende*. Or musicians. Or actors, when they* are *that character, and they are living that character, and something special happens in that moment…*

'I can't say any more.'

Salud

'He who tastes, knows.'

Proverb

CONTENTS

PREFACE	xi
EL SILENCIO	1
THE FIRST TIME	7
INTERVIEW I *On the UK publication of Duende*	11
NINETEENTH-CENTURY VIEW I *Gitanos*	17
THE NEXT PACO	23
OLD FLAMENCO SINGERS	29
A FLAMENCO DISCOGRAPHY	33
LA GUITARRA	37
A (SHORT) HISTORY OF FLAMENCO	43
INTERVIEW II *With the Italian newspaper La Repubblica*	47
FEMALE FLAMENCO GUITARISTS	51
THE GUITAR LESSON	57
POR SOLEARES *Traditional lyrics*	65
INTERVIEW III *With a Turkish newspaper*	71
FLAMENCO STYLES	77
CATCHING UP	83
PHOTO ESSAY Home-made Flamenco	89 91

¡AY!	105
OLÉ	111
NINETEENTH-CENTURY VIEW II *Triana*	115
THREE GREAT FLAMENCO GUITARISTS	121
FLAMENCO WEDDINGS	135
FLAMENCO AND SUFISM	145
INTERVIEW IV *With a Brazilian newspaper*	151
INFLUENCES	159
MUSIC FATIGUE	167
Y DESPUÉS	171
FINDING OTHER THINGS	177
A FLAMENCO GLOSSARY	183
A SPANISH REVIEW OF DUENDE	189
WHAT IS DUENDE?	193
Acknowledgments	199
About the Author	201
Request	203

PREFACE
THE ART OF FLAMENCO

This second volume in the *Mosaics of Spain* series returns to a subject which saw the launch of my writing career. *Duende: A Journey in Search of Flamenco* came out in the UK in early 2003 and went on to be translated into over a dozen languages, including Spanish.

The book told the story of certain powerful and sometimes difficult experiences which I had gone through as I moved towards adulthood. Not all of them happened in the sequence or context in which they appeared on the page, but the underlying thread which bound them together was flamenco. The writing of the manuscript itself had been a profound learning process for me, as the crafting of the disparate elements into a single narrative provided an important lesson about story-telling: how it has the power to heal by revealing overarching patterns and structures in our lives which can otherwise become hidden by over-emphasis on 'detail' or 'accuracy'. These qualities are often, in my view, confused with 'truth'. But this is not a topic which lends itself easily to discussion: reasoning is a world away from the kind of experience which leads to this way of seeing, and it was the very nature of my experiences in flamenco which had opened my eyes to this in the first place, for they showed me that parallel to the ordinary world there were other forms of existence which no words could describe. And that was the truth to which my first – and possibly only – loyalty lay: the book was an attempt to get as close to expressing it as I could.

Over twenty years have passed since I wrote the first draft. In that time, flamenco has continued to play an important part in my life as it led me to meet the woman who would become my wife. Salud still dances today, and continues to nurture a taste of the mysterious yet essential power which lies at the heart of the performance: *duende*. Watching members of the audience at the end of one of her shows, there is an unmistakable sparkle in their eyes, and expressions which speak of the curious, invigorating, even life-changing effect that *duende* can have. There is, for just a fleeting moment, a sense that, thanks to the dance and the music, the world and everything in it is just ever-so-slightly a better place, and that something of this understanding has been lodged in the hearts of those present. *Duende* is a reality, but has to be felt to be understood.

This current book, *The Art of Flamenco*, is not a continuation of *Duende*, however, for that story ended many years ago. It is, rather, a companion, a compilation of ideas and thoughts – some mine, some from others – centered around the art form and its essence. As with other volumes in the *Mosaics* series, it brings together multiple elements which, together, form a whole: a picture created by the arrangement of different pieces. Each one can, hopefully, be appreciated in its own right, while collectively creating something new.

It is, perhaps, just worth adding that – for me at least – impressions of flamenco and *duende* are intensely personal matters; they cannot be 'defined', as the more scholastically-minded might believe. In more recent years, with the increased amount of information available about flamenco and its official recognition by **UNESCO**, there appears to be a growing tendency to codify and even intellectualise the art form in certain circles. Doubtless these efforts bring some benefits, and flamenco as a whole is respected far more among ordinary Spaniards today than when I first encountered it over thirty years ago. Yet my firm belief is that its origins, essence and being lie in experience, and in experience alone. And that is something which, at best, intellect can only ever partially grasp.

Jason Webster

EL SILENCIO

EL SILENCIO

By Federico García Lorca

    Oye, hijo mío, el silencio.
    Es un silencio ondulado,
    un silencio,
    donde resbalan valles y ecos
    y que inclina las frentes
    hacia el suelo.

SILENCE

Listen, my son, to the silence.
It is a silence of waves,
a silence
where valleys and echoes slip by,
making us bow our heads
towards the ground.

THE FIRST TIME

THE FIRST TIME

A large woman stands up at the back of the stage and approaches the audience as the guitars play on. Raising an arm above her head, she stamps her foot hard, sweeps her hands down sharply to the side and stares at us in defiance. The music stops and everyone falls silent.

Power emanates from her across the square. Breathing hard, legs rooted to the ground, eyes bright, her face a vivid expression of pain. Everyone in the audience focuses on her as she stands motionless, leaning forward slightly, head thrust back, black hair falling loosely over her dark yellow dress. Stretching her arms, she tenses her hands open, as though receiving or absorbing some invisible energy. For a moment I think she might never move, need never move even, so strong is the spell she has cast over us. Then, slowly, she lowers her head till it rests on her chest.

A sound begins from somewhere, low and deep: a human voice resonating with complex harmonies locked into a single note. I assume it is coming from the stage, but the song – if song it is – seems to be unprojected, effortlessly filling the space around us like water. It shocks me, as if some long-dormant, primitive and troubled part of myself is being forced into wakefulness against its will. I have never felt anything like this before and struggle to comprehend as previously unfelt or forgotten emotions begin flowing through me, released by the trigger of the music. My eyes fixed ahead, I watch as the woman lifts her face once more, her mouth partly open, and I realise that the sound is coming from her.

She is singing. But there is no sweet voice, no pleasant melody, no recognisable tune at all. It is more like a scream, a cry or a shout. Behind her, the guitarists begin playing with short, rapid beats, fingers rippling over the strings in strange Moorish-sounding chords. The woman's voice lilts like a muezzin's call to prayer.

I am held by the music, as though any separation between myself and the rhythm has disappeared. An overweight woman singing on stage, dancing in a way that seems as if she is barely moving, yet I feel that she is stepping inside something and drawing me in with her. A chill, like a ripping sensation, moves up to my eyes. Tears begin to well up, while the cry from her lungs finds an echo within me, and makes me want to shout along with her. The hairs on my skin stand on end, blood drains to my feet. I am rooted to the spot, suspended between the emotion being drawn out of me, as though bypassing my mind, and the shame of what I am feeling.

The song continues and I become aware that others in the audience are experiencing the same. I can tell by the expressions on their faces, a certain look in their eyes, and simply feeling it sweep around us all in a second, like a trance. Then the cries begin as she finds the echo inside us: shouts of *Olé, Arsa, Eso es*. Some whisper under their breath, others shout, thick veins pulsating in their necks. The woman fills us, and the evening around us, with a sense of another space.

The song ends, and the audience breaks out into spontaneous, ecstatic applause. It is an emotional release, the greatest one might ever imagine. Pedro leans over to me.

'Did you feel it?' he asks.

From Duende: A Journey in Search of Flamenco

INTERVIEW I

ON THE UK PUBLICATION OF DUENDE

AN INTERVIEW ON THE UK PUBLICATION OF DUENDE

December 2002

How did you first become interested in flamenco?

I bought some second-hand tapes of the guitarist Carlos Montoya, and one or two things by Paco de Lucía, when I was a teenager. The music captivated me and seemed totally different to anything else I'd heard, with a power and passion that was hard to put your finger on. But it wasn't until I realised I wanted to go and live in Spain, in my early twenties, that my interest in flamenco began to flourish. It gave focus and meaning to what was then just a vague intuition that Spain was where my future lay.

Was it difficult for you to leave your life in England behind to live in Spain?

No. I took to the place immediately, as though I should have been there all along. The people were friendly and had a warmth about them I'd never found anywhere else. The language wasn't too difficult, the food was good and the weather was perfect. I immersed myself totally – probably too much.

What is 'real' flamenco, and where in Spain did you find it?

This is a very difficult question, and there is no definite answer. You can probably talk about three different layers of flamenco: people who live it in their homes, often Andalusians or Gypsies, for whom it is a kind of creed; good professional flamenco – performers like Paco de Lucía and Eva la Yerbabuena; and tourist flamenco – the kind of stuff you're likely to see on the Costas. Leaving the third category aside, there is a constant internal debate about what flamenco actually is and where it should be going. Roughly, there are two camps: the traditionalists and the innovators, the first treating it like a museum piece, the second sometimes experimenting so far they end up losing the plot. And each group accuses the other of killing the art form. In the end the answer has to do with *duende* – whether the performance has the special flamenco 'magic' in it or not. And each person you ask will have a different definition of what *duende* is. The nearest equivalent for English-speakers is when certain kinds of Afro-American music are said to have 'soul'. But really it's much darker and more powerful than that: a moment that has an almost primordial feel to it and an emotional intensity that can create a group trance effect.

As for where it can be found, the answer is: pretty much anywhere if you're in the right place at the right time. Having said that, it can be a frustrating search, as the top-rate stuff is rare, and is not always easy to appreciate for a first-time listener. Many Spaniards can't stand flamenco, and think it represents a backward and exotic view of the country held by foreigners which they themselves are keen to shake off. Nonetheless, it survives, and can hit you in the oddest moments: someone practising as you walk past a guitar-maker's shop, for instance, or schoolgirls singing and clapping a flamenco rhythm on their way home. My first experience of it was watching some enormous Gypsy women dancing one night in the main square in Alicante.

Were you surprised by what you found?

I hadn't really built up many expectations beforehand, but I remember being struck by the grace and vitality of these women, despite their being heavily overweight. It made me realise these qualities were much more than skin deep, that people can have all kinds of talents you wouldn't expect of them from first glance. And that flamenco, by accommodating this, had an uncommon authenticity about it. Then at a certain point in the gig came a *duende* moment and it changed my life, providing a driving force for my flamenco journey.

How difficult was it to learn to play flamenco guitar?

At first very difficult, as I had never really applied myself to anything in such a single-minded fashion before. But as time went on I became more and more obsessed with it, and would spend hour after hour practising, losing all sense of time. It was a necessary state to fall into if I was to make any serious progress, but one that proved to be quite destructive at the same time, as it started taking over my life. Too much music – either playing or listening to it – is probably not very good for you.

What kind of influence have your experiences in Spain had on your life now?

I spend most of my time in Spain, and my partner, Salud, is Spanish and a flamenco dancer. Beyond that, my experiences showed me all kinds of things about myself – some good, some bad – which otherwise might never have surfaced. Going down a path of emotional extremes meant I learnt a lot about my own passions, but coming out on the other side I realised it's not always such a good idea to be ruled by them.

NINETEENTH-CENTURY VIEW I

GITANOS

GITANOS

The following extract is taken from George Borrow's The Zincali: an Account of the Gypsies of Spain, *published in London in 1841*

The *Gitanos*, abject and vile as they have ever been, have nevertheless found admirers in Spain, individuals who have taken pleasure in their phraseology, pronunciation, and way of life; but above all, in the songs and dances of the females. This desire for cultivating their acquaintance is chiefly prevalent in Andalusia, where, indeed, they most abound; and more especially in the town of Seville, the capital of the province, where, in the *barrio* or Faubourg of Triana, a large Gitano colony has long flourished, with the denizens of which it is at all times easy to have intercourse, especially to those who are free of their money, and are willing to purchase such a gratification at the expense of dollars and pesetas.

When we consider the character of the Andalusians in general, we shall find little to surprise us in this predilection for the Gitanos. They are an indolent, frivolous people, fond of dancing and song, and sensual amusements. They live under the most glorious sun and benign heaven in Europe, and their country is by nature rich and fertile, yet in no province of Spain is there more beggary and misery; the greater part of the land being uncultivated, and producing nothing but thorns and brushwood, affording in itself a striking emblem of the moral state of its inhabitants.

Though not destitute of talent, the Andalusians are not much addicted to intellectual pursuits, at least in the present day. The person in most esteem among them is invariably the greatest *majo* [a 19th-century working-class 'chap'] and to acquire that character it is necessary to appear in the dress of a Merry Andrew, to bully, swagger, and smoke continually, to dance passably, and to strum the guitar. They are fond of obscenity and what they term *picardías*. Amongst them, learning is at a terrible discount, Greek, Latin, or any of the languages generally termed learned, being considered in any light but accomplishments, but not so the possession of thieves' slang or the dialect of the Gitanos, the knowledge of a few words of which invariably creates a certain degree of respect, as indicating that the individual is somewhat versed in that kind of life or *trato* for which alone the Andalusians have any kind of regard.

In Andalusia the Gitano has been studied by those who, for various reasons, have mingled with the Gitanos. It is tolerably well understood by the *chalans*, or jockeys, who have picked up many words in the fairs and market-places which the former frequent. It has, however, been cultivated to a greater degree by other individuals, who have sought the society of the Gitanos from a zest for their habits, their dances, and their songs; and such individuals have belonged to all classes, amongst them have been noblemen and members of the priestly order.

Perhaps no people in Andalusia have been more addicted in general to the acquaintance of the Gitanos than the friars, and preeminently amongst these the half-jockey, half-religious personages of the Cartujan convent at Xeres [Jerez]. This community, now suppressed, was, as is well known, in possession of a celebrated breed of horses, which fed in the pastures of the convent, and from which they derived no inconsiderable part of their revenue. These reverend gentlemen seem to have been much better versed in the points of a horse than in points of theology, and to have understood thieves' slang and Gitano far better than the language of the Vulgate. A chalan, who had some knowledge of the Gitano, related to me the following singular anecdote in connection with this subject:

He had occasion to go to the convent, having been long in treaty with the friars for a steed which he had been commissioned by a nobleman to buy at any reasonable price. The friars, however, were exorbitant in their demands. On arriving at the gate, he sang to the friar who opened it a couplet which he had composed in the Gypsy tongue, in which he stated the highest price which he was authorised to give for the animal in question; whereupon the friar instantly answered in the same tongue in an extemporary couplet full of abuse of him and his employer, and forthwith slammed the door in the face of the disconcerted jockey.

THE NEXT PACO

THE NEXT PACO

Spring 2015

Following the death of Paco de Lucía in February last year, the inevitable question is being asked about who is, or might eventually be, the next great flamenco guitarist – 'the next Paco'.

It is not an easy one to answer. Paco de Lucía casts a long shadow, while phrases like 'the next so-and-so' are lazy and rarely helpful. What's more, factors beyond an extraordinary talent also helped to usher in the musical revolution that Paco de Lucía was a fundamental part of. These included the presence at the time of other 'greats' (the singer Camarón de la Isla to name just one) and the enormous social changes that Spain was undergoing during the 1970s and 1980s. '*Nuevo Flamenco*' had much to do with the right people being in the right place at the right time. Perhaps not for several generations will anyone be able to bring about an equally powerful change in the art form.

Nonetheless, we can take a look to see who, if anyone, is pushing boundaries and keeping alive the spirit of experimentation that Paco de Lucía embodied. There are several candidates, but two names stand out at the moment: Miguel Angel Cortés and Dani de Morón.

For several years now Vicente Amigo has been mentioned as the carrier of the flame. Yet despite his technical brilliance and solid background, his work has rarely had the power to engage emotionally in the way of his predecessors. Crossovers between his music and the Chill-Out scene only seem to confirm his style as a kind of 'elevator flamenco' – pleasant enough, but sometimes unchallenging. Sadly, his latest recording – *Tierra* (2013) – shows little sign of change.

More recently, Manuel Parrilla, nephew of the Parrilla de Jerez who used to play with the legendary Paquera de Jerez, has finally recorded an album – *Pa Mi Gente* (2014) – after years of accompanying artists such as La Tati and Joaquín Cortés. Yet if something new and exciting were expected from a player who has grown up in one of the most important flamenco families, then there appears to be little evidence of it here. Parrilla's muscular style may work well when married to a dancer or singer, but on its own lacks texture and subtlety or even the playful sound we expect from Jerez, creating an album that at times becomes a little monotonous.

In contrast, Dani de Morón, a young player from Seville, continues to show that there is still much new ground to be broken and avenues to be explored. His 2012 album *Cambio de Sentido* demonstrated that a fresh and exciting talent had arrived on the scene, managing – as Dorantes has done in recent years on the piano – to push his instrument towards new territory while retaining flamenco depth – *jondura* – and avoiding the trap of straying into jazz. His next recording, when it comes, will be highly anticipated, but in the meantime have a look on YouTube for a *Seguiriya* he performed in Barcelona: it is one of the best renditions of this emotionally complex and difficult *palo* you can hear.

Another reason to be optimistic for the future of flamenco guitar is Granada-born Miguel Angel Cortés. Despite being something of a veteran – he played on Enrique Morente's groundbreaking 1996 album *Omega* – Cortés continues to mature. His multi-layered and highly polished album *El Calvario de un Genio* (2013) is one of the best recordings to have come out in the past couple of years and marks him out as one of the new stars.

And on the horizon? The 2013 album *Fluye* by José Quevedo 'Bolita' shows real promise, while others to watch out for in future include Jesús Guerrero, Santiago Lara and Eduardo Trassierra.

Paco de Lucía may no longer be with us, but what he helped to put in motion looks set to continue: as long as the new generation can step out from his shadow, the future for flamenco guitar looks bright. I hope, wherever he is right now, that the master is smiling at the prospect.

This article first appeared in Classical Guitar Magazine. *Since its publication in 2015, Vicente Amigo has brought out the album* Memoria de los Sentidos *(2017); Dani de Morón brought out an exceptional and highly recommended collaboration with some of the leading* cantaores – 21 *(2018); Miguel Angel Cortés,* Lo Cortés no quita lo Gallardo *(2015); Jesús Guerrero,* Calma *(2016); and Santiago Lara,* Flamenco Tribute to Pat Metheny *(2016).*

OLD FLAMENCO SINGERS

OLD FLAMENCO SINGERS

Luis Rosales (b. 1910) was a poet and essay writer from Granada, and a friend of Federico García Lorca. These are his comments on older cantaores *– flamenco singers:*

It's wonderful to listen to the older singers, to see them literally shouting themselves hoarse. Because nobody gives as much of themselves as singers who have lost their faculties. They sing to bring an end to it all. They sing as one should sing, with desperation and without malice, with a voice which no longer comes from the throat nor the chest, but from the whole body; a voice which hits notes by breaking them apart, but hits them nonetheless.

Sometimes it seems they sing by removing their voice from the note altogether, holding it merely with the breath. A singer like this is a prodigy, and the prodigy shows that while he still has a beating heart, his singing will survive. He doesn't need anything else.

And don't think that there is any mystery in this: it obeys a law. A flamenco singer always has to perform as though the singing itself could kill him, with the feeling that the true fullness of the singing can never be achieved. For that – which younger singers simulate by mere wheezing and panting – the older singers actually do: they *show* it, giving the song what I like to call its unfinished fullness.

A FLAMENCO DISCOGRAPHY

A FLAMENCO DISCOGRAPHY

*In 2004, I was asked (I can't remember by whom; perhaps by a magazine) to list my favourite flamenco records. I notice as I write this now (in 2020) that I would probably write the same, or very similar, list if asked today, only adding the flamenco recordings (*Los Ángeles *and* El Mal Querer*) of Rosalía, who is currently doing so much to shake up the world of flamenco, as well as the album* 21 *by the guitarist Dani de Morón*

OMEGA – Enrique Morente. The great Granadino sings words by García Lorca and Leonard Cohen to a flamenco and heavy metal backing track. Only Morente can do this. Wonderful.

MI CANTE Y UN POEMA – Estrella Morente. Enrique's daughter, and the great hope for the future of flamenco.

TAUROMAGIA – Manolo Sanlúcar. Virtuoso guitar playing inspired by the spectacle of the bullfight.

. . .

ALMORAIMA – Paco de Lucía. Anything by Paco is worth listening to. This is a classic of *Nuevo Flamenco*.

POTRO DE RABIA Y MIEL – Camarón de la Isla. His last album, and possibly his best. The deification of Camarón is quickly turning into an industry, but listen to him singing *por bulerías* and you'll understand how special he was.

A MANDELI – Pepe Habichuela. Simply great flamenco guitar.

OROBROY – Dorantes. Others have tried to play flamenco piano, but it sounds like jazz. Dorantes manages to pull it off, sounding almost like a flamenco version of Satie.

JEREZ CANTA POR BULERÍAS – Various. Just for the sense of fun they put into the music. Real fiesta stuff.

ESQUILONES DE PLATA – La Niña de los Peines (Pastora Pavón Cruz). Perhaps my favourite flamenco track. Raw and passionate. It can be found on various compilation records.

UN RAMITO DE LOCURA – Carmen Linares. Beautiful, mournful singing accompanied by the masterful Gerardo Núñez.

MORDIENDO EL DUENDE – Mártires del Compás. Of all the bands of *Nuevo Flamenco*, these guys sound the most authentic: rough-edged and unique.

LA GUITARRA

LA GUITARRA

By Federico García Lorca

    Empieza el llanto
    de la guitarra.
    Se rompen las copas
    de la madrugada.
    Empieza el llanto
    de la guitarra.
    Es inútil
    callarla.
    Es imposible
    callarla.
    Llora monótona
    como llora el agua,
    como llora el viento
    sobre la nevada.
    Es imposible
    callarla.
    Llora por cosas
    lejanas.

Arena del Sur caliente
que pide camelias blancas.
Llora flecha sin blanco,
la tarde sin mañana,
y el primer pájaro muerto
sobre la rama.
¡Oh guitarra!
Corazón malherido
por cinco espadas.

THE GUITAR

The weeping of the guitar
begins.
The empty glasses of dawn
are smashed to the ground.
The weeping of the guitar
begins.
Useless
to silence it.
Impossible
to silence it.
It weeps ever the same song
like the weeping of water,
like the weeping of the wind
over snow.
Impossible
to silence it.
It weeps
for what lies afar.
Hot southern sands
crying out for white camellias.
It weeps for the arrow with no target,

the evening with no morning
and the first bird to die
in the tree.
Oh guitar!
a heart wounded
by five piercing swords.

A (SHORT) HISTORY OF FLAMENCO

A (SHORT) HISTORY OF FLAMENCO

There is no certainty about when flamenco began. The 18th and 19th centuries are often cited as the period when it started to take shape. But the Roman poet Juvenal referred to Cádiz girls in Rome – *puellae gaditanae* – who performed dances with bronze castanets in the time of the emperor Trajan. For the poet and flamencologist Domingo Manfredi this is evidence enough to date flamenco back to classical times.

'No scientific argument is necessary to understand that those dancers, those singers, taken to Rome from Cádiz... sang and danced Andalusian dances and songs which wouldn't be very different from those performed today,' he says.

Others are less certain. Manuel de Falla suggested a multiple origin, highlighting the Moorish invasion of Spain in 711, the Spanish church's adoption of the Byzantine liturgical chant, and the arrival of the Gypsies from Europe in the 15th century, bringing with them enharmonic influences from Indian songs, as the key factors in the development of the art form.

The role of the Gypsies is crucial but perhaps the least understood. First there is the question of when they actually did come to Spain. There appear to have been at least two waves: one from North Africa during the Islamic period, and another from France in the years shortly before the fall of Granada in 1492. That they have played a major role in the development of flamenco is not in doubt; the question is to what extent. Are they its sole creators? If so, why aren't there more obvious echoes in Gypsy music from other countries? Did they just take already existing folk songs and transform them with their own interpretation and style? Some have tried to divide *palos* into those of supposedly Gypsy and non-Gypsy origin, with a *bulería*, for example, being placed in the Gypsy category, and a *fandango* labelled as 'Spanish'. Others categorise certain *palos* as being outside flamenco altogether. *Sevillanas*, the essence for most foreigners of 'typical Spanish' flamenco, with their castanets and dancers in long-tailed frilly dresses, would be classified by most aficionados as 'folklore', not as flamenco.

Such matters belong in the realm of 'flamencology', though, where the more scholarly minded spend hours arguing over finer points of detail in a manner reminiscent of medieval monks and their angels on pin-heads.

For most *flamencos*, these things are intuited, if thought about at all. Moorish or Jewish, Gypsy or Andalusian, there is an instinctive feel for flamenco, making it easy to recognise, if difficult to define. It's something about being away from the mainstream, on the outside. For the past two hundred years at least, flamenco has been the music and dance of outcasts, people on the margins of Spanish society. Hence the natural affinity with Gypsies, and a large number of songs about injustice or imprisonment:

> *Don't come crying*
> *to the prison bars;*
> *since you can't ease my pain*
> *don't come here making it worse.*

The only certainty about flamenco is that it began in Andalusia and remains to this day Andalusian, despite its spread across Spain and around the world. Madrid, and to a lesser extent Barcelona, have become flamenco centres, but only by importing southern communities and culture. Andalusia, with its poverty, arid heat and proximity to Africa, remains the eternal reference point and true source.

INTERVIEW II

WITH THE ITALIAN NEWSPAPER LA REPUBBLICA

AN INTERVIEW WITH THE ITALIAN NEWSPAPER LA REPUBBLICA

November 2003

Why did you choose duende *as your subject for this book?*

Duende is a kind of 'magic' which can ignite a flamenco performance, usually when there is a kind of special energy between the players and the audience. Each person you ask will have a different definition of what *duende* is.

I chose to write about it because of a series of powerful and life-changing experiences I had in Spain during my twenties. I moved there after leaving university, nursing a broken heart from a failed relationship with a girl in Florence – a city where I spent a lot of my formative years. In Spain I quickly became obsessed with the strange, almost Oriental sounds of flamenco and immersed myself in it, finding a passion there and in the people around me that I felt had been lacking in my life. What I didn't realise at the time, though, was that I was embarking on a very dangerous journey – complete with drugs, theft, a gun-wielding jealous husband and the death of a friend – from which I was lucky to come out in one piece. By taking stock of what had happened to me and learning from some of the lessons I had been through, the book *Duende* emerged.

How much is duende *a part of your life?*

I was obsessed with flamenco and with *duende* for a long time, and it gave me a lot, but also proved to be painful in many ways. For that reason now I treat it with more respect. *Duende* is part of my life and always will be, because it is partly responsible for who I have become, but I don't think about it, or flamenco, as much as I used to. Writing the book was a way of drawing a line under certain experiences. I play the guitar at home with my wife, Salud, a flamenco dancer, but that's it. It's a good way to relax when you're writing. But I listen to far less music in general these days. Getting in touch with your emotions is all very well, but it's not an end in itself.

Are you writing a new book? Could you tell me something about it?

I've just finished writing another book – *Andalus, Unlocking the Secrets of Moorish Spain* – published in England in spring next year. I've always been fascinated by the Arabs and their influence on Europe. So much of Western culture actually derives from the Moors, yet we tend to think of it only as a combination of Christianity and the Classical world. Spain – and Sicily, obviously – are very interesting examples of where European and Islamic cultures came into close contact and actually fused together in some way. So I went on a journey around Spain and Portugal looking for remnants of the Moorish past – the language, food, music and people. For much of the way I was joined by an illegal Moroccan immigrant who saved my life when I went to investigate a farm where he was working in conditions of semi-slavery. We had a series of Quixotic adventures as we travelled together, and these turned into the material for the book.

FEMALE FLAMENCO GUITARISTS

FEMALE FLAMENCO GUITARISTS

Summer 2015

Women's rights, like democracy, came relatively late to Spain. Franco's 'National-Catholicist' regime held back social reforms: divorce was only finally legalised in 1981, and abortion as recently as 2010.

So it should come as no surprise that the world of flamenco has rarely been a bastion of equal opportunities, particularly given its close links with the socially conservative Gypsy community. This has been most apparent among guitar players; until now, female guitarists – *tocaoras* – have always existed as a tiny, uncelebrated minority.

There are many reasons for this, but of the three pillars of the art form – dance (*el baile*), singing (*el cante*) and guitar (*el toque*) – guitar-playing is the only one where a gender difference makes no difference, turning a woman performer into a potential threat to male dominance.

Female guitarists, however, have existed probably for as long as flamenco itself. The Victorian British travel writer George Borrow mentions an unnamed woman guitarist resident in the jail of Toro in his classic book *The Bible in Spain*. In the early 20th century Adela Cubas, Victoria de Miguel (who was taught by Andrés Segovia), Paca *la*

Coja and Trinidad Huertas, *La Cuenca*, were all well known and highly regarded players.

Franco's Civil War victory in 1939 brought great social change, however, and female guitarists became less prominent over the second half of the 20th century as a result. Happily for us, this trend is now waning, and we can talk about a great leap forward for *tocaoras* in recent years – although it is interesting to note that to a significant degree this new movement is coming from outside Spain or from non-Spanish players.

Among native Spanish guitarists, the most important name at present is Antonia Jiménez, from Puerto de Santa María. Now in her forties, Jiménez has accompanied singers such as the great Carmen Linares, Montse Cortés or the young and award-winning Juan Pinilla from Granada. She has also been at the centre of the critically acclaimed show *De Flamencas*, a homage to female performers by the celebrated dancer Marco Flores. In addition, Jiménez has gone on to create her own production, *Dos Tocaoras*, in conjunction with Marta Robles, a classically trained guitarist from Seville who has concentrated more recently on flamenco.

Other Spanish players of note at present include: Pilar Alonso, who studied under Manolo Sanlúcar and is 'Spain's first official female flamenco guitar teacher'; Laura González; Mercedes Luján; and Celia Morales, who has her own school in Ronda.

Interestingly, however, the first woman guitarist to record an album lives not in Spain, but in Montreal. Caroline Planté's *8Reflexiones* came out in 2010 and is a treat. Taught from a young age by her father Marcel, Planté shows total mastery not only of her instrument, but of the many different *palos* of flamenco. The album combines sounds from rap and African music, and fits well into the mould of 'flamenco-fusion' that has been in vogue for so long now. But the moments of pure flamenco are the ones that stand out, with Planté's performance showing both subtlety, great accompanying skill (not least on the track with singing star Duquende), as well as unique flair. Let's hope a follow-up album won't be too long in coming.

Another 'foreign' player who has taken a similar, if even less orthodox, route is Bettina Flater from Norway, who combines songs in her native language with her guitar playing in two albums to date:

Women en Mi (2012) and *La Gota y La Mar* (2014). Personally I admire her courage, and the results are interesting, but the marriage of flamenco and Norwegian song is not always successful and in some instances upstages her undoubted skill as a guitarist.

Continuing the trend of non-Spanish players challenging perceptions about female guitarists is Noa Drezner. Born in Israel but based in Jerez, Drezner has a great future ahead of her. Still in her early thirties, she has partnered Antonia Jiménez in *De Flamencas* and was one of the most exciting talents to appear in Alicia Cifredo's documentary on female flamenco guitar players, *Tocaoras* (2014). She tours regularly in Israel, where she is a soloist with the Israeli Andalusian Orchestra of Ashdod. She is currently working on her debut album.

After years of prejudice, today, female flamenco guitarists are undoubtedly on the rise and becoming noticed (a book about them, *Mujeres Guitarristas* by Eulalia Pablo Lozano was published in Spain in 2009). In fact, as Drezner says, it can even be an advantage to be a woman in a male-dominated world, as the strangeness of being a *tocaora* can attract more attention and publicity. The numbers are still small, and there is a feeling of sisterhood among many of them. But we will only know that real progress has been been made when articles such as this are no longer written, and male and female guitarists are mentioned in the same breath, with no reference made whatsoever to their gender.

This article first appeared in Classical Guitar Magazine. *Since its publication in 2015, Noa Drezner has brought out her first album,* El Hilo Rojo *(2019).*

THE GUITAR LESSON

THE GUITAR LESSON

'Flamenco is organic. A living thing which will become your life-force... if you practise hard enough.'

It was late afternoon and I was sitting in Juan's red flat: red walls, red floors, red chairs, red table, red curtains hanging over red windows.

'Red is the colour of flamenco,' he would say. 'The colour of passion.'

He served coffee from a red pot into red cups which we stirred with spoons with red handles. Everything, from the corridor to the bedroom to the bathroom, was red. The toilet paper, however, was pink.

'Yes,' he said, looking a little disappointed when I pointed this out. 'They don't make it in red.'

The flat was a temple to flamenco. Pictures of past greats stared down at us from the walls: the singer La Niña de los Peines with her thinly pencilled eyebrows and heavy, bad-tempered face; the dancer La Argentinita, the flamenco muse of the 1920s and 30s who inspired Manuel de Falla to write his famous *El Amor Brujo*; and Ramón Montoya, the first *flamenco* to develop the guitar as a solo instrument, fat and immaculately-dressed as the previous generation of *flamencos* always had been. Juan had placed old guitars in corners, or hanging from the walls, as if he needed constant reminding of who he was. I couldn't be sure if it was reflected light, but I could have sworn some of them had a red tinge in the varnish.

Juan spent most of the first lessons guiding me through the array of flamenco objects dotted around his flat. It seemed to please him to have someone to show off his memorabilia to, and for the time being I went along with it, happy to delay the serious business of starting to play in earnest. I told him I could barely hit a note and was coming to flamenco with hardly any musical knowledge; a plea, I suppose, for him not to expect too much. Despite his friendliness I could sense there was a fierce temperament in him and a moodiness which I wanted to avoid as much as possible.

Flamenco played all the time. Juan had hundreds, possibly thousands of records and CDs and an entire wall was taken up by a sophisticated stereo system. Which was black: luckily there were no red ones on sale. He seemed to spend most of his time buying expensive pieces of kit which he could add on to it, producing some crucial improvement in the sound quality. I could never tell the difference myself, but he always swore by his gadgets.

And when not playing the guitar, he was usually tapping out some complicated rhythm with his fingers, flicking them out one by one with amazing dexterity and independence of movement. Invariably as I walked into his house for a class, a new recording was blaring as he wrapped his knuckles in time on the counter like a typist.

'Have you heard this?' he would shout enthusiastically above the music. 'It's the latest from Carmen Linares. I met her once. Nice woman. I love her singing.' At this point I would put down the guitar and head to the kitchen to pour myself a glass of water.

'The cables for the speakers are new – made of gold,' he would shout through. 'It gives a purer sound. More heart. More love.' And he pounded the centre of his chest while looking up at the red ceiling.

The music only stopped for our lessons, when my fumbling on the guitar demanded silence and Juan's reluctant attention. For all his love of flamenco, he rarely seemed keen to teach me. He would rather spend the time talking – about a particular guitarist or singer, or mostly about new pieces of equipment. 'Hey, have a look at this electronic tuner. Fantastic. Tells you exactly when you're in tune.'

Each time it was a challenge to get the lesson started. No longer childishly enthusiastic, he would, as I had half-suspected, become surly and moody.

'Look, boy. You're not even holding it properly. Concentrate.'

We started at the very beginning. During a handful of classes I had taken before leaving England I had been taught the traditional posture, with the guitar resting on the left or right leg, pointing diagonally upwards to aid access for the left hand. But the contemporary style was to cross the legs, right over left, and hug the guitar into the hip, tilting it away from the body, so that the fret board was almost invisible and you relied on touch and familiarity alone. This put a strain on the muscles in the left arm at first, stretching them into a strange position, and the right hand constantly suffered from pins and needles as the forearm rested too heavily on the edge of the guitar. It took months to perfect.

'Work on it. You've got it totally wrong,' Juan barked. Then, in a rare moment of compassion, he added, 'It's worth it. It gives you a more relaxed feel. And more importantly...' He lowered his voice and I leant forward to catch his words of wisdom, 'You look really cool.'

It was hard to feel cool while contorting my body into what seemed like the most unnatural position imaginable. Admittedly it didn't look that difficult, as I gazed at myself in the full-length red-framed mirror on the wall, but the strain on my arms and wrists was excruciating. I'm going to be permanently crippled at this rate, I thought. My body felt frozen in the act of playing; even outside the class my right hand fell into a 'telephone' position: little finger sticking out for balance and thumb bent back, as though resting on the bottom string, middle fingers bent into the palm slightly. I took to shaking it like a rattle to try to loosen the muscles and tendons.

'Your hands are too stiff,' Juan would moan. 'Too hard. Relax that wrist. Here, feel my hand.'

It felt like a freshly killed chicken: warm, limp, not quite all there.

'Today we're looking at the *bulería*,' he said one afternoon when I'd finally persuaded him to teach me something. Flamenco, I was slowly realising, was far more than simply the energetic beat of the Gypsy Kings or ornate singing and playing. It was a world in itself, with its own lexicon and rules. There were scores of different *palos*, each with a unique feeling based on variations in key, rhythm and pace. Regional styles created an extra level of complication, with major differences between, say, a *fandango de Málaga* and a *fandango de Murcia*.

'*Bulería*. It comes from *burlar*. It means to joke around, make fun of someone. It captures something essential, the essence of flamenco. You listen to a good *bulería*, and you feel like you hardly know where the rhythm is going next, they keep playing with it all the time. But they always stay religiously within the rules. It's a type of magic. Takes years to get to that stage.'

I had listened to him playing *bulerías* and they fascinated me with their manic, restless beat, impossible to follow at this early stage unless he counted out loud, helping me understand the complicated rhythm. It had a Gypsy feel to it: anarchic, unpredictable, weaving in and out as though you might never catch hold of it.

'This is the real thing, boy: what we always play at *juergas* – flamenco parties,' Juan said. 'I suppose you expected to learn all that Gypsy Kings stuff, eh? Simple *rumbas* to show off to the girls? Look, if you want to learn with me we start with the most difficult things first. Got it?'

We sat opposite one another in the red haze. Juan was looking at me – how I sat, the positioning of the guitar. He seemed about to say something, a look of reproach on his face, but instead checked himself and glanced down at his own guitar.

'You already know the rhythm.'

He played, his fingers moving with great speed, and a hypnotic sound filled the room. It seemed so effortless, I simply listened in amazement, my eyes and attention wandering over the faces on the posters around us. It still surprised me sometimes that I was here in Spain having lessons with a real flamenco guitar teacher. Only a couple of weeks previously I thought I had made a disastrous choice in coming to Alicante to begin my search, but I had suddenly landed on my feet and now things were moving faster than I could take them in.

Juan stopped with a flourish. I stared. I had no idea what he had just done. But he was glaring at me.

'Come on!' he growled. 'Your turn!'

I felt a knot tightening in my guts. Do what, exactly? I had no idea what he had just played.

'Umm...' I stammered.

'Concentrate, boy. If you're going to take this seriously I expect you to watch *every* move I make like a hawk. I play, you watch, you learn. That's how it goes.'

I nodded in agreement, silently wishing I were somewhere else. Sweat began to trickle down my neck.

'Now watch! I'll do it again. But understand that I'm being nice to you. Don't expect me to play things for you twice in the future.'

This time I leaned forward over my guitar, straining my eyes in an attempt to follow his fingers as they danced over the strings like a carpet-weaver's. The problem was how to divide my attention; there was as much happening with his right hand as there was with his left, and try as I might, I couldn't watch them both at the same time. In the end I concentrated on the left – reasoning that at least I might be able to get the chords. The right hand would have to come later.

Juan finished the piece and then stood up.

'OK boy. Now you do it.'

He walked into the kitchen to light a cigarette – Marlboro, they had the reddest packets, he said – and started heating some water for coffee.

'And work on your right hand. The left will look after itself.'

I sat desperately over the guitar. My fingers formed into what looked like an approximation of what I had seen him do. The forefinger was bent in some strange position covering two strings at the same time. I felt a shot of pain as it was forced back against itself while the strings underneath cut into the skin from the pressure. Wincing, I looked up. Juan's back was turned.

'Come on! I can't hear anything.'

I gritted my teeth and started strumming with my right hand. There was a horrible dead sound. I readjusted my fingers on the fretboard, and the pain shot up my arm as the soft tips were sliced by the strings. Juan, now standing in the doorway, was looking at me sternly. I swallowed an urge to give up and pressed on. There was a small improvement – sound coming from at least three strings. But my fingers were raw and I let them drop.

'Eh! What are you doing? Come on! Next chord.'

I placed my hands again where they had been, hoping that they would automatically remember what came next. But they let me down. I sat, flustered, my mind blank, Juan's eyes burning into the top of my head as he stood over me. His foot was tapping, but I couldn't tell whether it was impatience or just another rhythm working its way in his mind. My face turned red, like everything else in the flat.

'Come on, boy.'

With my fingers slipping over the ebony board, I tried as hard as I could to remember how he had placed his hand. Like this? No, bring that finger down. One more fret. There. I hit down with my index finger and waited for the cacophony and the bark of reproach that would inevitably follow. I stopped. It sounded vile. My head stayed bent over the guitar. There was silence for a minute, then finally Juan spoke.

'Well?' he said, cigarette hanging from his mouth. 'What are you waiting for? Do it again! Come on. *Compás*! Rhythm! One, two, THREE, four, five…'

I fumbled to catch up with his clapping. Unbelievably, I had got it right. But it sounded so horrible. Was that how it was supposed to be? But there was no time for questions. Juan was driving me on, and I had to catch up.

From Duende: A Journey in Search of Flamenco

POR SOLEARES

TRADITIONAL LYRICS

POR SOLEARES

Traditional lyrics sung in Andalusian dialect to the slow, melancholic flamenco style known as *Soleá* or *Soleares*, from the Spanish word *soledad*, meaning 'loneliness'

>Tú eres la estrella del Norte,
>la primera que sale
>la última que s'esconde.
>
>Levántate tempranito
>y verás cómo te traigo
>de yerbagüena un ramito.
>
>Tu ventana es una carse
>con el carselero dentro
>y el prisionero en la calle.
>
>Vente conmigo a un parmá,
>y te cogeré parmito
>y tú te los comerá.

Arrímate a mi queré
como las salamanquesas
s'arriman a la paré.

Qué quieres que tenga:
que m'han dicho que tu cuerpo
se lo va a comer la tierra.

Compañera, si me muero
la casilla de los locos
ha de ser tu paraero.

Diez años después de muerto
y de gusanos comío
letreros tendrán mis huesos
der tiempo que t'he querío.

El letrero de mi puerta
dice a quien sepa leer:
por aquí salgo con ella
o por aquí no saldré.

Er que me quiere quitá
er querer d'esta gitana
ha de matarse conmigo
debajo de su ventana.

POR SOLEARES

You are the North Star,
the first to shine
the last to go out.

Early in the morning, when you wake,
you will see how I shall bring you
fresh sprigs of spearmint.

Your window is a prison,
but the gaoler is inside
while outside waits the prisoner.

Come with me to a palm grove,
I'll scoop out palm hearts
for you to eat.

Press yourself to my love
like a salamander
flattens itself against a wall.

What do you expect me to feel?
They say your body
will be eaten by the earth.

My beloved, if I die
your final destination
will be the mad house.

And after ten years in my grave
being eaten by worms,
my carved bones will spell out
all that I loved you.

The sign on my door
tells all who can read:
either I leave here with her
or I won't come out at all.

For anyone who tries to take from me
the love of this Gypsy girl
will die with me first
outside her window.

INTERVIEW III

WITH A TURKISH NEWSPAPER

INTERVIEW WITH A TURKISH NEWSPAPER

July 2004

In Turkey, there has always been a belief that Turkey is a country connecting East to West. But we never thought East met West in Spain too. Do you consider Spain as such a country?

Very much so. The Moors were in Spain for almost a thousand years. And here the impact of East and West coming together had a much greater impact on the development of European culture. The Renaissance would never have got off the ground in Italy had it not been for the caliphs of Córdoba.

In the old times Westerners went to Kathmandu or similar Asian destinations. Why did you choose Spain as the starting point of your journey.

'Westerners' have travelled all over the place at almost all times. I think you're referring to the hippie trails of the 60s and 70s. There is a much longer tradition of people leaving their homelands to explore different cultures and civilisations. Ibn Battuta and Ibn Jubayr were trailblazers of this in the Islamic World; Marco Polo here in Europe. I went to Spain simply because it seemed to ring some inner bell, as if I knew intuitively it was the place I had to go to.

I am sure you are familiar with the Arabic word 'vecd'. Do you think vecd *is similar to* duende*?*

Turkish spellings of Arabic words always confuse me a bit. I'm more aware of the term '*hal*', but this is, I believe, a specific word used in mystical circles. Does flamenco have a mystical element to it? I'm not sure. It's very emotional, and I don't think the two things are the same. I suspect on balance that flamenco can produce emotional experiences in people which they find odd and incredibly intense, and so they reach out for other words to describe what is happening to them.

It is always the East creating concepts or lifestyles like duende *and* vecd*. Why do you think the West is not able to do this?*

Well, *duende* is a Western concept, in that you find it here in Spain. But I understand what you mean. I think it probably dates back to the 18th century, when Europe passed through its 'Age of Reason'. Rational thought became supreme and anything deemed 'irrational' was rejected. Accordingly, if something cannot be scrutinised or observed using the 'scientific method' it simply doesn't exist.

You elaborately and extensively described the gardens there. Maghribis [Moroccans, or Muslims of the western Mediterranean] turn their gardens into their lifestyle. What sort of difference do you see between British gardens and Maghribi gardens?

. . .

I'm not an expert on gardens. I remember once someone explaining to me, however, the difference between British and Italian gardens. Italian gardens, he said, represent Man's efforts to shape nature as he wishes it to be. British gardens, however, work with nature, trying to bring out the better qualities, say, of a particular landscape, rather than forcing it to conform to some preconceived ideas about what a garden should look like. If anything, I think Moorish gardens and British gardens have something similar in this regard: bringing out the inherent beauty within nature itself.

Gypsies: they refuse to be a State [sic], they refuse institutionalization, they also don't show any national characteristics, they don't have a common Gypsy culture. The only characteristic they share is being Gypsy, and music and flowers. Still they are the heart of flamenco? Why do you think so?

Very difficult question. Much of flamenco has nothing to do with Gypsies, and many Spanish Gypsies know almost nothing about flamenco. That said, however, they are at the heart of the art form, as you say. In the end I think it has something to do with being on the edge of society. Flamenco has always been a music of people on the fringes, outcasts. This may be why flamenco is going through a bad patch at the moment, in my opinion. Successful *flamencos* in the past never lost that 'edginess' and sense of not belonging to mainstream society. Nowadays they are paid huge amounts of money and are living far too comfortably, I think, to be able to produce the real thing. The rawness of the music has to come from a certain harshness of life.

You preserved your Western language and attitude. You could have used a language characteristic to Gypsies, flamenco and underground, but you did not? Any special reason?

My attitude is my own. Neither Western nor Eastern. And my language is English. What did you want me to do? Write the book in Caló?

There are Gypsy words and phrases in the book if you want them, but in the mouths of Gypsies who appear in it.

You seem to have avoided sex scenes. Your definition of such passionate moments are quite reserved, quite Western. If there was a duende *moment when making love as well, why did you not include that in the book? Don't you think it would have been a great idea to create* duende *in that area as well?*

You obviously haven't been to the West for some time. You can't move here for sex. Our culture is obsessed with it. Perhaps for that reason I wanted to 'draw a veil' over certain scenes. Sex is always sexier when something is left unsaid.

Lola character seems a bit too weak. Do you have any special reason for that?

Did I deliberately make Lola a weak character? Strange question. Answer: No.

What did all these experiences leave behind on you? Was that a temporary touristic interest or were there any permanent influences?

My experiences were never 'touristic'. I lived in Spain for three years, and now I'm back again. Spain has touched me profoundly, and I feel more at home here than anywhere else.

FLAMENCO STYLES

FLAMENCO STYLES

Flamenco music is divided up into several styles, know as *palos*. Each *palo* has its own distinctive feel and emotion, with certain associated chords, lyrics, rhythms and dance moves. Many have a particular link with certain Andalusian cities: *verdiales*, for example, come from Málaga, while *granaínas* are part of Granadan culture, as their name suggests. Others, for example *bulerías* and *tango*, are an integral part of flamenco Gypsy tradition. Together they form a kind of family which, as a whole, makes up the flamenco repertoire.

The following is a beginner's guide to what are generally regarded as the most important or most common styles, arranged in alphabetical order.

Alegrías – A happy and upbeat fiesta style, as the name describes. Has a quick, twelve-beat rhythm and is usually accompanied by dance. Musically, most flamenco is played in the distinctive Phrygian mode (in which a C scale starts on E). *Alegrías*, however, are played in the more normal Ionian mode, making them sound more 'familiar' to many non-Spanish ears.

. . .

Bulerías – One of the most commonly heard styles at a Gypsy fiesta. The twelve-beat *bulería* is often played at breakneck speed, with a complex and seemingly incomprehensible under- and overlay of polyrhythms producing an often-hypnotic effect. Over the past thirty or forty years it has become one of the most popular *palos*, with artists drawn to its energy and flexibility.

Fandangos – The *palo* with the greatest number of variants according to where its performers hail from. *Fandangos* are thought to have originated in the Americas, from where they penetrated Spanish culture – probably via the port city of Cádiz – and took on local characteristics. Flamenco *fandangos* (*Fandangos aflamencados*) have a three-beat rhythm and have become a standard style.

Tangos – As with *fandangos*, *tangos* appear to have originated in the Americas, from where they reached Spain – again through Cádiz. What became known as *tanguillos* developed in the city as a very popular and jocular style of singing with a distinctive 'galloping-horse' rhythm which can also be heard in North African music. This later evolved into a slower *palo* known as *tientos*, which in turn became the quicker four-beat *tangos* that we know today (although some contest this theory). Along with *bulerías*, they are among the most popular fiesta styles.

Seguiriyas – This *palo* is venerated as one of the oldest and 'purest' within the flamenco family. Its slow, dramatic rhythm probably originated as a song or chant used by mourners at funerals. Along with *solerares*, it is considered one of the most important styles that make up the 'deep song' (*cante jondo*) – the richest and most mystical form within flamenco. It can easily be recognised by the singer's frequent use in the song of the Spanish lament: *¡Ay!*

. . .

Soleares – Often known as 'the mother of flamenco', the *soleá* is a slow and melancholic *palo* with a twelve-beat rhythm that is considered to be the cornerstone, or the 'marrow', of 'deep song'. If there is one style capable of producing an experience of *duende* in the listener, then it would be this, with its unmatched emotive and almost transcendental melodic qualities.

CATCHING UP

CATCHING UP

'Of course it all started with Paco and *Almoraima*,' Eduardo said one evening as we sat under the palm trees drinking *horchata* – tiger-nut milk – on the breezy Esplanade. Never one to understate things, I had the impression he was about to pass down some important information.

'What started?' I asked tentatively.

'Paco de Lucía. 1976.' I was puzzled. 'He brought out *Almoraima* in 1976 and that was it. *Bam*! He reinvented flamenco. It was dying, dead, before then.'

Paco was a big name: the father of the new sound. He had taken the ideas of players from the previous generation – Sabicas and El Niño Ricardo – and transformed them, introducing new elements from jazz and rock. Now probably the best-known *flamenco* on the planet, he had an ever larger following outside Spain after his collaboration with John McLaughlin and Al di Meola in the 80s. Almost every contemporary flamenco guitarist owed a debt to him in their playing, so great the impact he had in what for many was the revolution he had spearheaded over the previous two decades. He had his critics: people who thought the music had been sacrificed for technique. But they were a minority. Most aficionados revered him and his new records were always eagerly awaited to see if the great master was about to point a new direction for the rest to follow.

'What do you mean, dead?' I retorted. 'What about all the people before him? Carlos Montoya...'

'Carlos Montoya? Don't make me laugh. Have you ever heard Carlos Montoya?'

'Yes, I...'

'*Ese no vale una mierda!* Crap. Can't play to save his life. You listen to his *compás*, it's all over the place. Can't keep rhythm. I tell you, if he were – if he were playing today he'd be laughed off the stage.'

'Oh, come on! You mean everyone who's playing now is better than him?'

'Yes.' His answer was so abrupt and confident it was impossible to argue.

'You need to be listening to a lot more stuff if you're still on Carlos Montoya, son. Tomatito, Gerardo Núñez, Pepe Habichuela – these are the guys you've got to get hold of.'

I had to concede. I still knew too little about it all to start arguing with a real aficionado. Besides, it would be a sign of even greater weakness to admit I couldn't hear the supposed flaws.

'Listen son, if you're interested in flamenco as you say you are, you've got to learn everything about it. Got to turn yourself into an expert. You can't be ignorant all you life.' I nodded.

'Anyway,' he said, 'you'll find out soon enough: flamenco does strange things to you.'

Over the following weeks I learnt as much as I could from my new flamenco guru. Juan would teach me how to play, but it was Eduardo who would tell me all there was to know about the contemporary scene: who to listen to, who to avoid, why such-and-such a player was so important, the lesser-known guitarists some of the greats had taken their ideas from. From here it was a full-on flamenco course: my day was taken up either playing the guitar, with Juan, listening to tapes lent to me by Eduardo, or hearing him talking about it into the early hours. He would often come to the flat unnanounced for a tutorial, or we would meet at a café on the sea front before moving to the late-night bars in the barrio. His obsession was far greater than anything I had come across amongst Lola's group of friends, who, I soon realised, were mere amateurs by comparison. Eduardo could talk endlessly, and loved nothing better than to have me as his disciple, a new convert to the cause in a world which, in his eyes, was appreciating real flamenco less and less.

'Paco may be the leader of the pack, but a lot's down to his dad. He had this plan to take over flamenco. Tried to turn all five kids into professional players or *flamencos*. Almost succeeded – his only failure is the second son – ended up working in a hotel in Madrid, or something.' He waved for two more beers.

'Don't get me wrong: Paco's a genius, greatest player of his time. But, well, has he gone too far? That's the question.'

'Too far in what?' I asked.

'Too jazzy, son, too jazzy. Here, how much flamenco are you listening to?'

'Um…'

'It's just that his latest stuff's just straying a bit too far for my liking. Some people love it. So do I. Love it. But is it still flamenco? I don't know. For me, well… It's his early stuff that's just brilliant, just brilliant. Of course, some say he just nicked all his ideas from others like El Niño Miguel. But you hear them playing, and you know, you can just tell, Paco's just storming. Amazing.'

'You can tell them apart, then?' Still drowning in ignorance, I took a punt on what sounded like a more educated question.

'Course, son. *Por supuesto*. Much earthier sound, not all there. But he didn't have the contacts. Not like Paco. No wonder he never made it big. He's poor and forgotten now.'

There was another 'great' in modern flamenco, though. Eduardo revered him even more than Paco.

'Camarón de la Isla.' His voice would go all soft and wobbly just at the name. But I found it hard to get enthusiastic about someone called the *Shrimp of the Island*.

'The greatest singer there's ever been. Anywhere. Other singers can do it sometimes, but he, he…' His eyes would go all strange at this point, mad and staring.

'Do what?'

'It, son. It. *Duende*.'

I sat up. Yes, what did Eduardo think of *duende*? What was it?

Slowly he pulled a tape from his pocket and handed it to me.

'Go home and listen to this.'

Back in the flat I put the tape on. Camarón had a much higher voice than I'd expected from the photo on the front cover: a light-haired man with a saurian face and bright, emotional eyes. But as soon as it began I could understand Eduardo's devotion. He had a unique voice that conveyed a gut-twisting, tragic sorrow. Even when singing happier pieces – an *alegría* for example – there was the unmistakable melancholy and agony in his voice. And from what Eduardo told me he was an explosive character: a Gypsy and the hard man of flamenco whose life reflected the passion of his art. It was widely suspected that he was an alcoholic and drug addict. And perhaps predictably he had died young. He had been the greatest *flamenco* of his generation.

'A man like that only comes once every hundred years,' Eduardo told me when I handed the tape back. 'There might never be another one like him. This is a Golden Age, a Golden Age, I tell you. Catch it, because it's going to end soon.'

From Duende: A Journey in Search of Flamenco

PHOTO ESSAY
HOME-MADE FLAMENCO

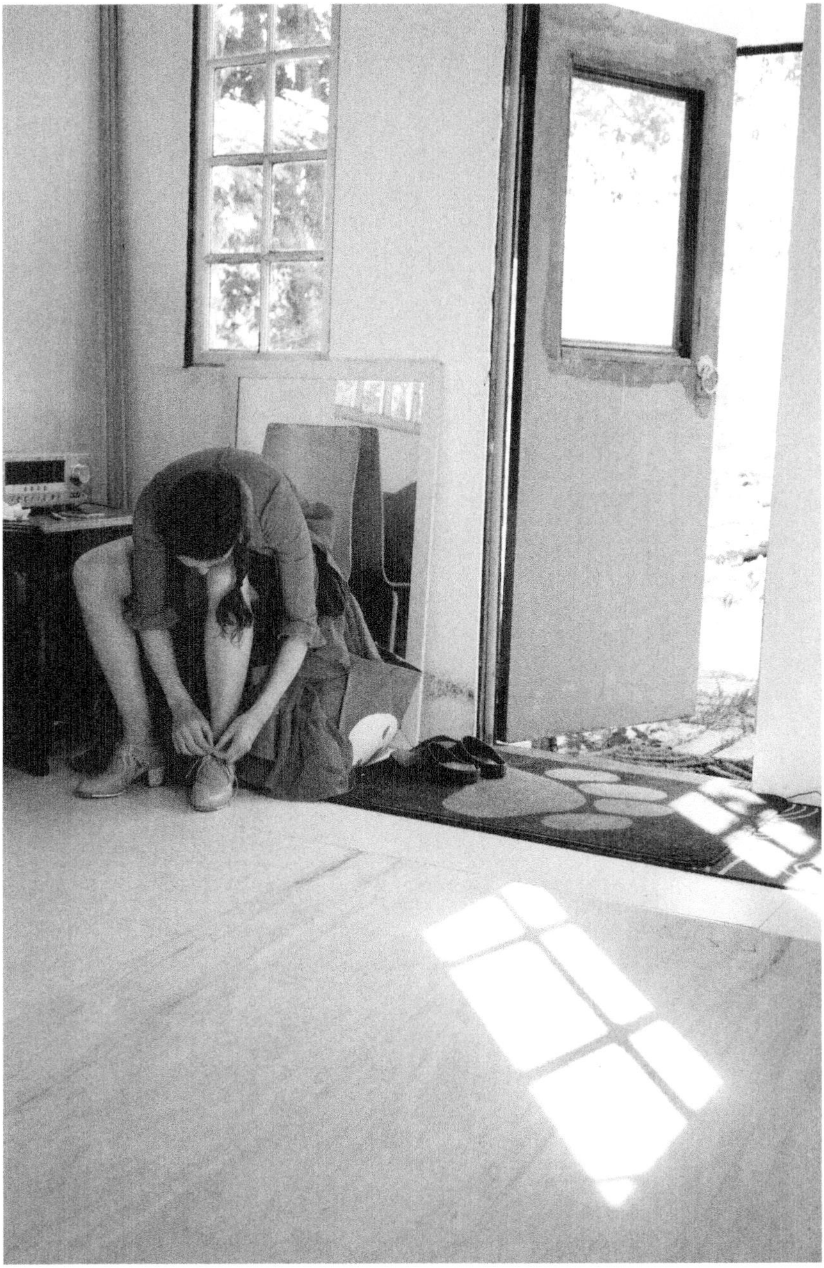

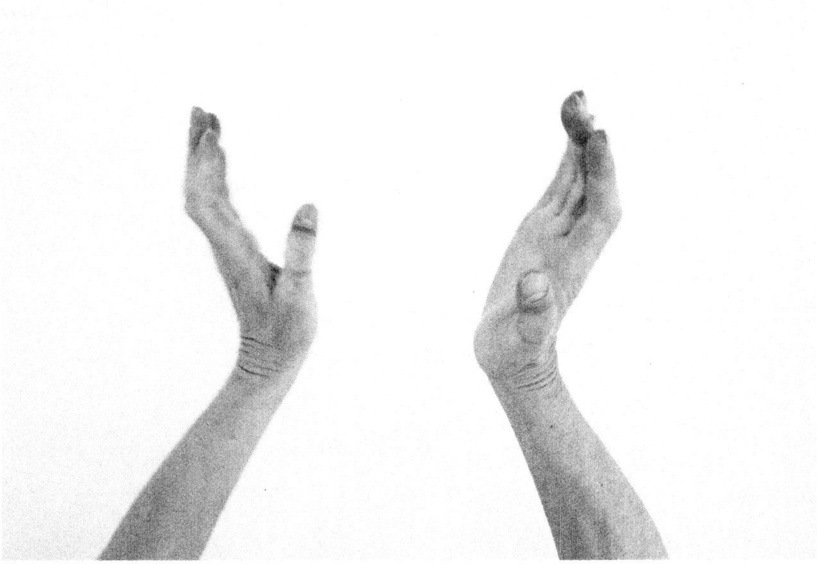

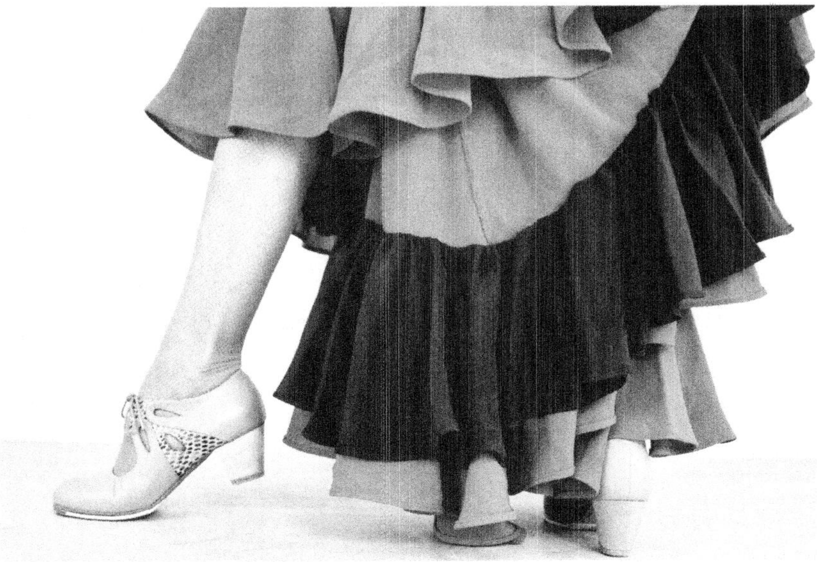

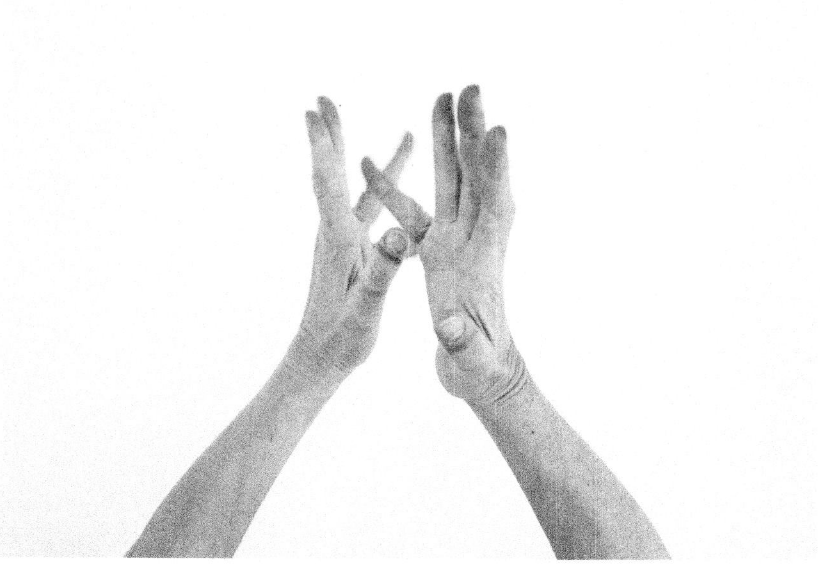

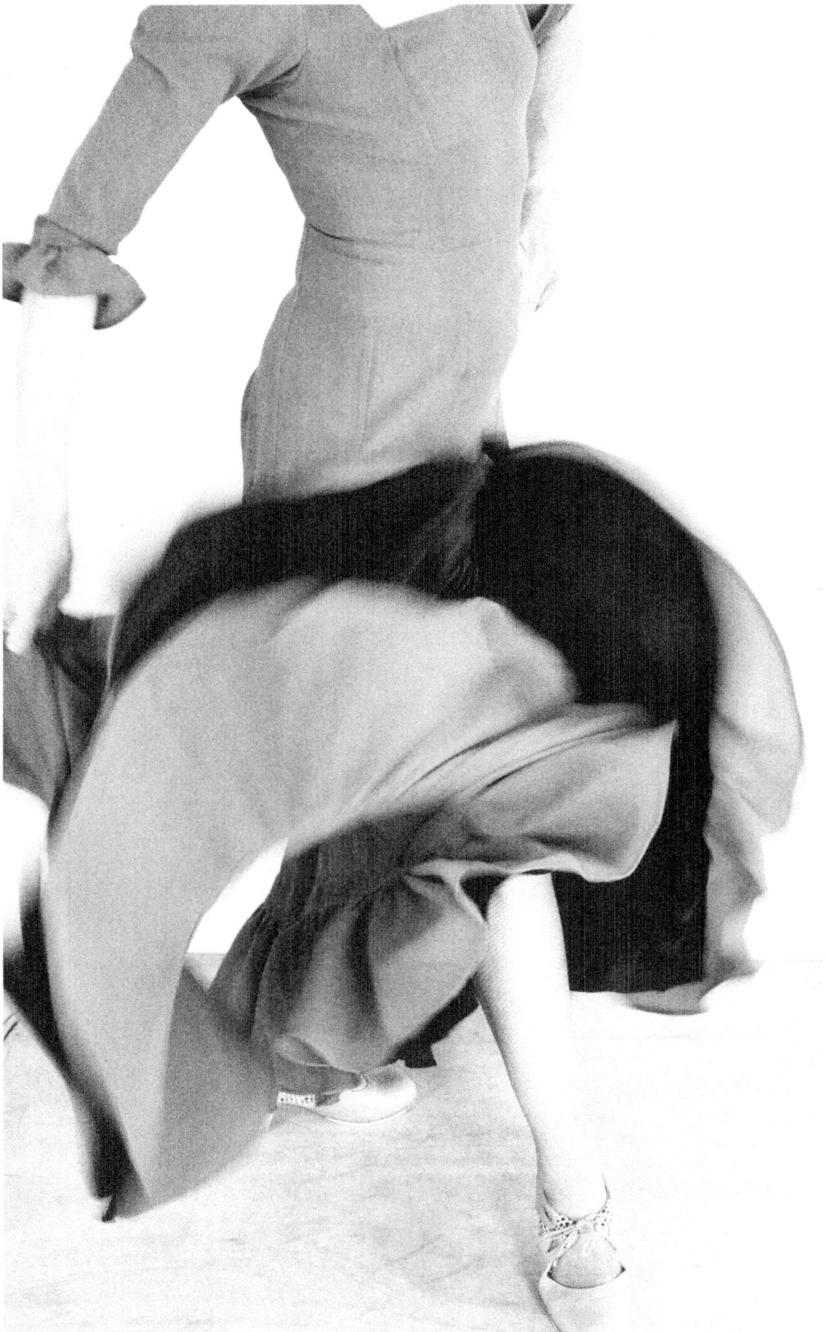

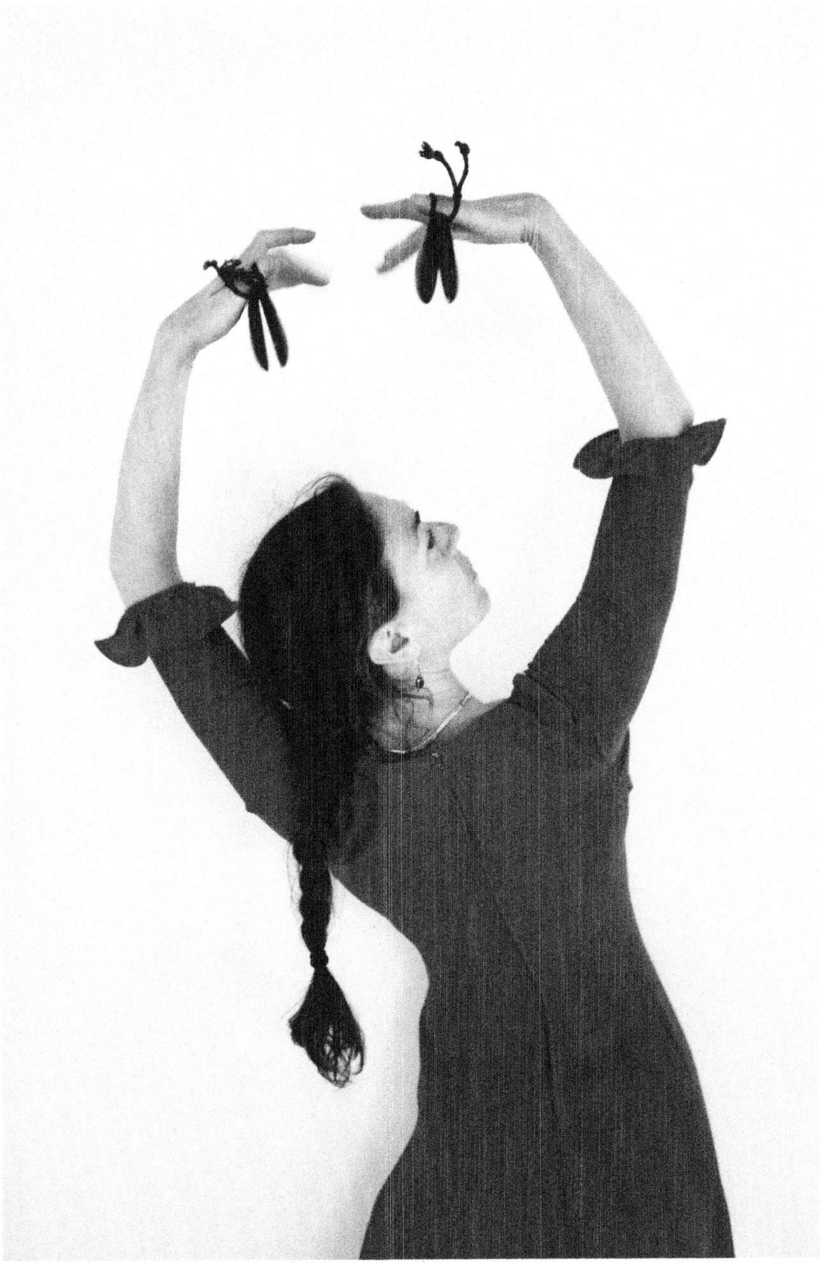

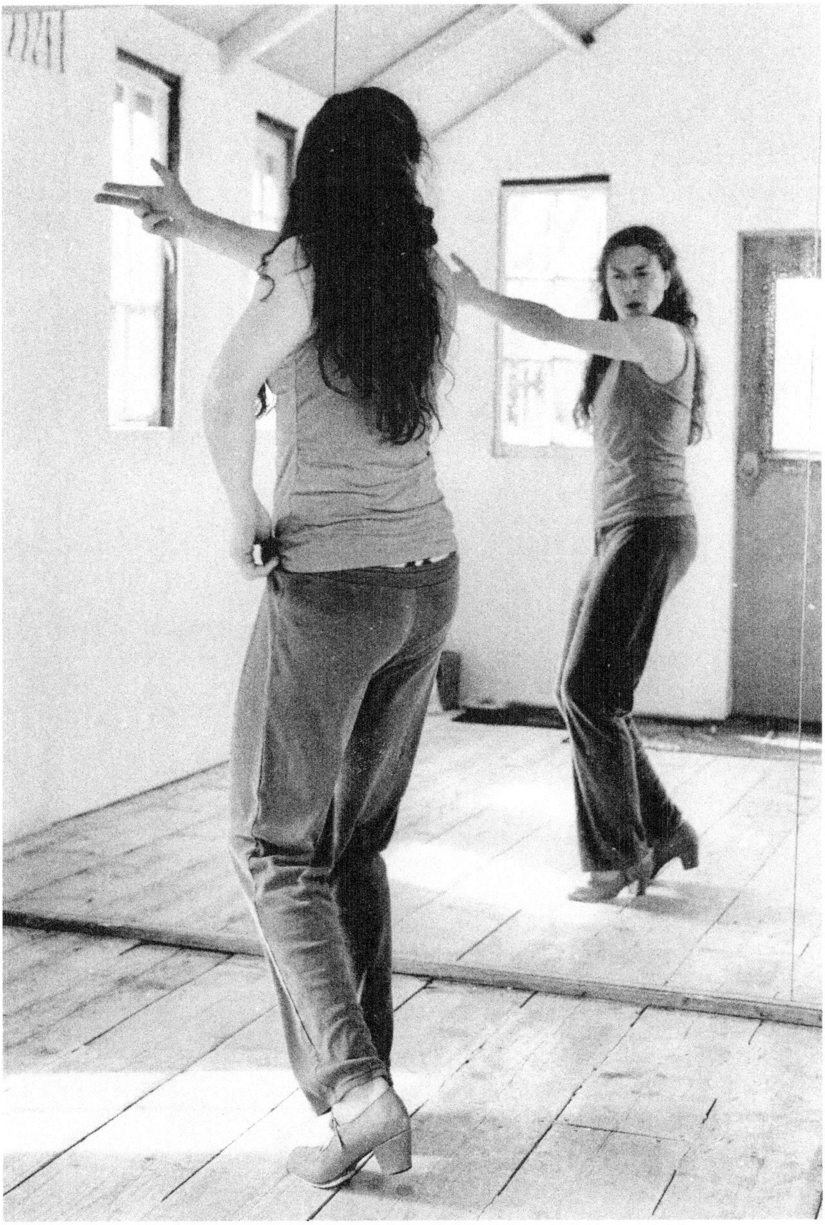

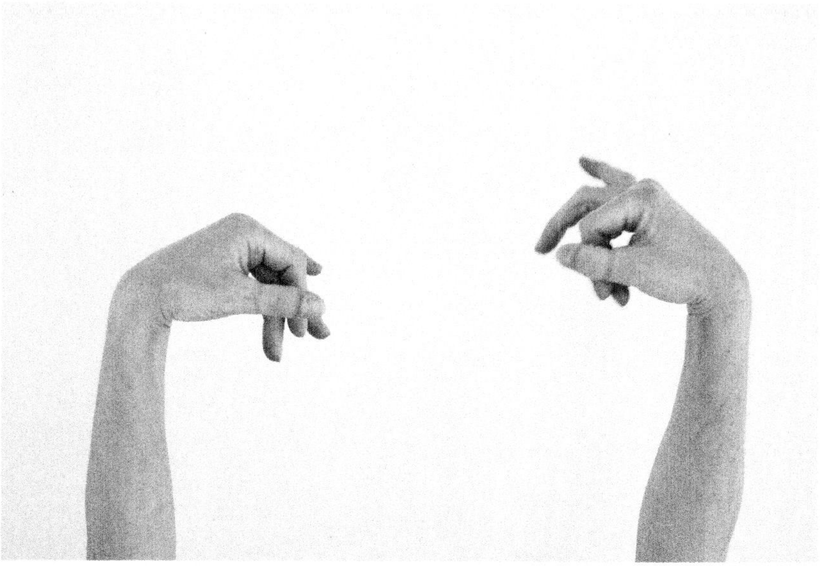

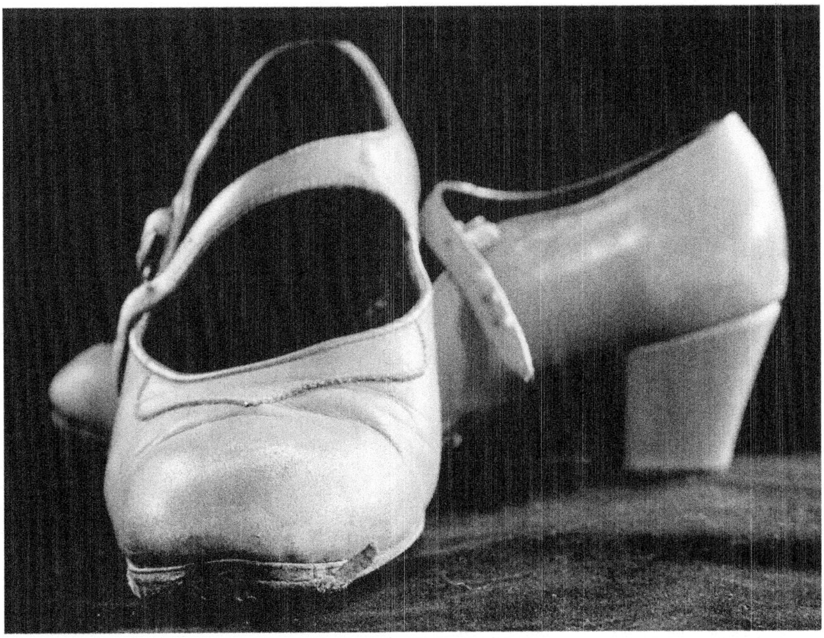

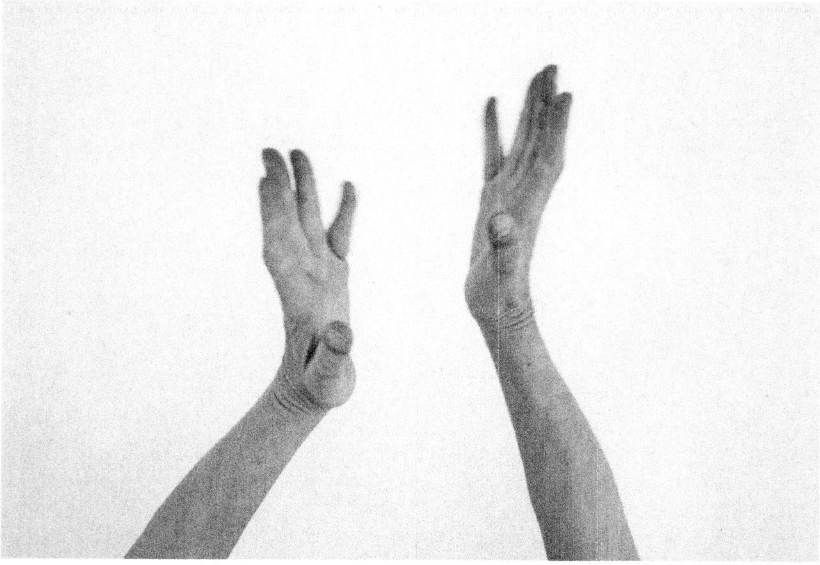

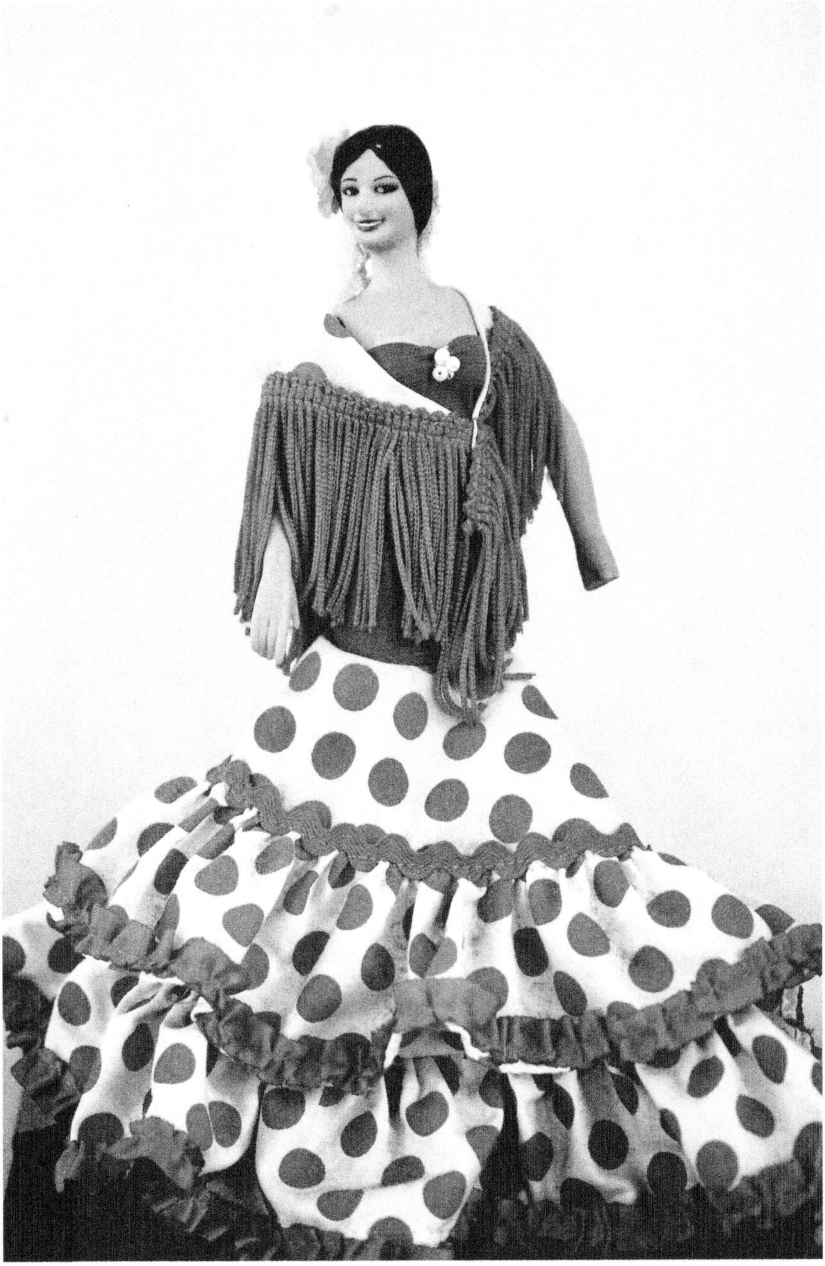

¡AY!

¡AY!

By Federico García Lorca

El grito deja en el viento
una sombra de ciprés.

(Dejadme en este campo
llorando.)

Todo se ha roto en el mundo.
No queda más que el silencio.

(Dejadme en este campo
llorando.)

El horizonte sin luz
está mordido de hogueras.

(Ya os he dicho que me dejéis
en este campo
llorando.)

¡AY!

The cry leaves the shadow of
a cypress tree in the wind.

(Let me weep alone
in this field.)

Everything in the world has broken.
Nothing remains but silence.

(Let me weep alone
in this field.)

The dark horizon is being eaten
by fire.

(I told you to leave me
alone in this field
weeping.)

OLÉ

OLÉ

My voyage of discovery around Moorish Spain had just begun, but I was already back home and the only thing I'd managed to pick up was an out-of-work Moroccan. I felt honour-bound to find Zine a job, and was genuinely concerned about him, but I was wondering how my journey was going to get off the ground. I kept my eyes open for clues in my search, but for the moment it looked as though Musa's treasure would have to wait. The problem was, I wasn't sure for how long.

'¡*Hala!*' The cries from the women in the church echoed out again.

'Listen,' said Zine, leaning over to me and pointing. 'What are they saying?'

'*Hala*,' I said. 'It's a common expression of surprise.'

It was a word I'd used myself hundreds of times. But for some reason, perhaps because I was talking to an Arab, that night in the square its significance suddenly became clear, and I remembered something: like that most Spanish of words *olé*, it sounded remarkably like the Arabic *Allah*. That must have been its origin. I recalled hearing something similar not long before: the Arabic '*in sha' Allah*'. Zine had said it in the car: 'God willing'. Muslims used it all the time when talking about the future. The phrase had been adopted into Spanish as *ojalá* as a way of expressing hope: friends who had travelled into the Amazon jungle told me you even heard Native Americans using it.

Allah was used in a whole host of Arabic expressions: '*yallah*', meaning 'let's go'; '*ma sha Allah*', 'amazing'; or often just *Allah* on its own, much as Westerners might exclaim 'God!'. If '*in sha' Allah*' had been adopted into Spanish, I couldn't see why *Allah* on its own hadn't as well: the Spanish '*Hala*' sounded the same.

I mentioned my idea to Zine.

'They're saying *Allah*?' he said with a dramatic expression of surprise on his face.

Salud was more interested in what looked like a street-theatre performance taking place on the other side of the square, great flaming torches lighting up a scene of colourfully painted faces and fantastical costumes.

'*Olé*,' I said trying to catch her attention. 'That comes from Arabic, too, from *wallahi* – 'By God'.'

She walked on.

'In Andalusian churches,' I explained to Zine, 'you often hear them shouting ¡*Olé!* Imagine that: the name of the God of Islam being used in a Christian church. But the participants don't even realise.'

I laughed. A fascination was developing in me for such things: for me they were clues in my attempt to understand Spain's unique character: a culture which, if my suspicion was right, appeared to have been formed by two ostensibly opposed religions. I felt like I'd unexpectedly stumbled on an important piece of evidence, one that had been staring me in the face for years. Yet Salud, as Spanish as ever, had yet to be infected by my enthusiasm for her country's Moorish past.

'So?' she said. '*Olé* is *olé*. They're not Muslims.'

As a flamenco dancer the word belonged to her, the emotive cry of *olé* being an essential part of any good performance. It didn't do for me to try to take it away from her.

'Yes, I know. But isn't it amazing…'

'They don't know they're saying *Allah*. It's just *olé*.'

Zine patted me on the back.

'I heard you,' he said.

From Andalus: Unlocking the Mysteries of Moorish Spain

NINETEENTH-CENTURY VIEW II

TRIANA

TRIANA

Richard Ford journeyed extensively through Spain at a similar time to George Borrow (whose The Zincali *provides other extracts in this book), and wrote a celebrated* Handbook *for English-speaking travellers to the country. Here are his thoughts on Gypsy dance and music, taken from his* Gatherings From Spain, *published in London in 1846:*

But in Spain at every moment one retraces the steps of antiquity; thus still on the banks of the Bætis [Gualdalquivir] may be seen those dancing-girls of profligate Gades [Cádiz], which were exported to ancient Rome, with pickled tunnies, to the delight of wicked epicures and the horror of the good fathers of the early church, who compared them, and perhaps justly, to the capering performed by the daughter of Herodias. They were prohibited by Theodosius, because, according to St. Chrysostom, at such balls the devil never wanted a partner. The well-known statue at Naples called the *Venere Callipige* is the representation of Telethusa, or some other Cádiz dancing-girl. Seville is now in these matters what Gades was; never there is wanting some venerable Gipsy hag, who will get up a *función* as these pretty proceedings are called, a word taken from the pontifical ceremonies; for Italy set the fashion to Spain once, as France does now. These festivals must be paid for, since the Gitanesque race, according to Cervantes, were only sent into this world as 'fishhooks for purses'. The *callees* when young are very pretty – then they have such wheedling ways, and traffic on such sure wants and wishes, since to Spanish men they prophesy gold, to women, husbands.

The scene of the ball is generally placed in the suburb Triana, which is the Transtevere of the town, and the home of bullfighters, smugglers, picturesque rogues, and Egyptians, whose women are the premières danseuses on these occasions, in which men never take a part. The house selected is usually one of those semi-Moorish abodes and perfect pictures, where rags, poverty, and ruin, are mixed up with marble columns, figs, fountains and grapes; the party assembles in some stately saloon, whose gilded Arab roof – safe from the spoiler – hangs over whitewashed walls, and the few wooden benches on which the chaperons and invited are seated, among whom quantity is rather preferred to quality; nor would the company or costume perhaps be admissible at the Mansion-house; but here the past triumphs over the present; the dance which is closely analogous to the *Ghowasee* of the Egyptians, and the *Nautch* of the Hindoos, is called the *Olé* by Spaniards, the *Romalis* by their Gipsies; the soul and essence of it consists in the expression of certain sentiment, one not indeed of a very sentimental or correct character. The ladies, who seem to have no bones, resolve the problem of perpetual motion, their feet having comparatively a sinecure, as the whole person performs a pantomime, and trembles like an aspen leaf; the flexible form and Terpsichore figure of a young Andalusian girl – be she gipsy or not – is said by the learned, to have been designed by nature as the fit frame for her voluptuous imagination.

Be that as it may, the scholar and classical commentator will every moment quote Martial, &c., when he beholds the unchanged balancing of hands, raised as if to catch showers of roses, the tapping of the feet, and the serpentine, quivering movements. A contagious excitement seizes the spectators, who, like Orientals, beat time with their hands in measured cadence, and at every pause applaud with cries and clappings. The damsels, thus encouraged, continue in violent action until nature is all but exhausted; then aniseed brandy, wine, and *alpisteras* [a sweet pastry] are handed about, and the fête, carried on to early dawn, often concludes in broken heads, which here are called 'Gipsy's fare'. These dances appear to a stranger from the chilly north, to be more marked by energy than by grace, nor have the legs less to do than the body, hips, and arms. The sight of this unchanged pastime of antiquity, which excites the Spaniards to frenzy, rather disgusts an English spectator, possibly from some national malorganization, for, as Molière says, '*l'Angleterre a produit des grands hommes dans les sciences et les beaux arts, mais pas un grand danseur—allez lire l'histoire.*' However indecent these dances may be, yet the performers are inviolably chaste, and as far at least as un-Gipsy guests are concerned, may be compared to iced punch at a rout; young girls go through them before the applauding eyes of their parents and brothers, who would resent to the death any attempt on their sisters' virtue.

During the lucid intervals between the ballet and the brandy, *La caña*, the true Arabic *gaunia*, song is administered as a soother by some hirsute artiste, without frills, studs, diamonds, or kid gloves, whose staves, sad and melancholy, always begin and end with an *ay!* a high-pitched sigh, or cry. These Moorish melodies, relics of auld lang syne, are best preserved in the hill-built villages near Ronda, where there are no roads for the members of Queen Christina's *Conservatorio Napolitano*...

THREE GREAT FLAMENCO GUITARISTS

MANUEL MOLINA

The past few years have seen the deaths of a significant number of the greats of flamenco, musicians who revolutionised the art form, helped propel it into the future and defined a generation. Among them are internationally renowned figures – Paco de Lucía and Enrique Morente perhaps being the most celebrated. But May this year saw the passing of one *flamenco* possibly less famous outside Spain, but who, at the peak of his popularity, used to hire Paco de Lucía as his support act for sell-out performances in football stadia and bullrings around the country. That man was Manuel Molina, guitarist, singer, composer, lyricist, 'flamenco troubadour', free thinker and one half of the chart-topping duo of the 1970s, Lole y Manuel.

No flamenco guitarist understood the power of silence like Molina. While soloists around him were forever speeding up, seeming to fit more notes than was physically possible into a bar, Molina's music was as content speaking the language of pause, alongside the choppy virtuosity that defined his playing. Visually, he was an arresting performer, holding the guitar vertically – not unlike Picasso's *Old Guitarist*, but with his head turned in towards his instrument rather than away from it. Pioneering his own unique style of accompanying song and dance, and absorbing influences as diverse as traditional Moroccan rhythms and the psychedelic blues-rock of Jimi Hendrix, he was one of the prime movers of what became known as *Nuevo Flamenco*, the thrilling experimentation of the 1970s which made flamenco a bestseller once more and provided the soundtrack for a generation finally casting off the chattels of the Franco dictatorship.

Molina was born in 1948 in the Spanish North African enclave of Ceuta. His father was a Gypsy flamenco guitarist known as El Encajero. When he was still young, the family moved across the Strait to the Spanish mainland and the coastal city of Algeciras, where Molina first met an adolescent Paco de Lucía. 'He was always busy studying the guitar then,' he later said of him.

Before long, however, Molina was on the move again, finally settling in Seville, which remained his home for the rest of his life, and became the city with which he most identified.

'A person can be from wherever he wants to be,' he once said, in a comment that typified much of the freedom of spirit that defined his character.

A chance to join the rock band Smash helped get him out of military service (the lead singer had good contacts), which was when Molina started mixing different musical styles with flamenco. In time this would become known as 'flamenco fusion'; Molina was there at the start, but tended not to use the term himself, preferring to speak of 'blending' or 'learning'.

Real success, however, came when he started performing with Lole Montoya, daughter of the Gypsy flamenco singer La Negra. Artistic as well as marriage partners, together they formed Lole y Manuel, one of the most successful musical duos in modern Spanish history. While Molina experimented with new rhythms, Lole sang with a clearer, more melodic voice than was common at the time, combining the flamenco aesthetic with a hippie flavour that became an instant hit with young Spaniards who until that moment had regarded flamenco as the music of the past. The couple's first album, *Nuevo día* (1975), came out just as Franco was dying and encapsulated much of the heady, hopeful spirit of the period, not least with its title.

'We want to make flamenco not only show its sad side,' he once said, 'but its life-loving one as well: flowers, sunshine and all those vital qualities needed to understand the Andalusian people.'

More albums followed at the rate of one a year, but by the 1980s the marriage had ended and their artistic collaborations continued only sporadically. Nonetheless, the impact had been made, and flamenco would never be the same again.

Molina continued to play, either singing to his own guitar playing or accompanying dancers such as Farruquito and Manuela Carrasco. International recognition of sorts came when a Lole y Manuel track – *Tu Mirá* – was used in Quentin Tarantino's film *Kill Bill 2*. A couple of months before he died, Molina was diagnosed with terminal cancer. In a gesture characteristic of the man, he decided to forego any medical treatment.

'Money,' he said, 'is the real cancer. And the rest – lack of understanding, power, egoism – is the metastasis.'

Joyful, independent and unique, he died in much the way that he lived – uncompromising, quintessentially flamenco, and always forging his own path. No one better could write his epitaph:

> *Let no one cry the day I die;*
> *It's more beautiful to sing,*
> *Even if the song comes with pain.*

He leaves us with a legacy based as much on words as on his playing.

MANOLO SANLÚCAR

No overview of the past forty years of Spanish guitar would be complete without an appreciation of Manolo Sanlúcar, co-instigator of the late 20th-century revolution in flamenco music. Like many leading figures in the art form, Manuel (Manolo) Muñoz was brought up in a flamenco family, born in the coastal town of Sanlúcar de Barrameda near Cádiz in 1943. His father was a guitarist who used to play with the legendary singer Pepe Marchena. The young Manolo was taught by his father from an early age, making his professional debut when he was only thirteen. In his early career he was supported by La Niña de los Peines and was for a long time accompanist to singer La Paquera de Jerez, a powerful, thunderstorm of a *cantaora* who marked a turning point in Manolo's artistic development. It is commonly said that a flamenco guitarist needs to spend ten years accompanying dancers and another ten with singers before he should play solo. Manolo did his full apprenticeship and, adopting the stage name 'Sanlúcar' after his home town, he started playing concerts and recitals across Spain, where his unmistakable talent, clean sound and technical virtuosity made him quickly stand out as someone to watch.

It was the early 1970s and Spain was entering a fascinating transitional phase socially, politically and culturally. The Franco regime was in its death throws and old taboos were being broken. Like many of his contemporaries, Sanlúcar started to experiment with his art form, pushing it in new directions, extending its boundaries. As he himself later commented: 'We realised that the guitar needed to be harmonically enriched; flamenco guitar [at the time] was harmonically impoverished.'

Some of his exploration moved in the direction of 'easy listening' and pop, heralded by his track *Cabello Negro* on his 1974 album *Sanlúcar*. With its use of drums, electric bass and rhythm guitars, it was one of the milestones in the development of what later became known as *Nuevo Flamenco*. This was followed several years later by the hit tracks *Candela* (1980) and *Al Viento* (1982).

Apart from this lighter sound, Sanlúcar's greatest legacy will perhaps lie in his marriage of flamenco with classical music, a format in which he shines both as composer and virtuoso. This relationship began with his *Fantasía para guitarra y orquesta* (1978), an ambitious four-movement piece with clear influences from Joaquín Rodrigo and the Spanish classical guitar tradition. This was followed in 1982 by his 'flamenco opera' titled *Ven y sígueme*, in which the singers El Lebrijano and Rocío Jurado performed, and his ballet *Medea*, which has been taken around the world by the Spanish National Ballet Company.

As with all flamenco greats, however, Sanlúcar is engaged in the complex balancing act between innovating and remaining loyal to tradition and, while forays into the classical world have opened new possibilities, he has never forgotten his roots. The synthesis that this has produced in his music is best represented by *Tauromagia* (1988), one of his masterpieces and, in my opinion, possibly the best flamenco guitar album ever recorded. The music charts the course of a bullfight, from the animal's life in the countryside, to the beginning of the fight, the pageantry and various sections of the *lidia*, and finally the torero's triumphal exit through the main gate. The *bulería Tercio de Vara* has a subtlety, balance and complexity to it that alone makes the entire album worth listening to, while the final track, *Puerta del Príncipe* has become one of Sanlúcar's signature pieces and featured in Carlos Saura's celebrated film *Flamenco*.

After performing such great service to flamenco, scoring huge successes and winning countless awards, in 2013 Sanlúcar announced at the age of seventy that he was retiring. He has not played in public since, but leaves a rich legacy, not only in the new territory he explored for the art form, but in the large number of younger players who have been inspired – directly and indirectly – to follow in his footsteps. If you don't know his work, go out and discover it – you have a treat waiting for you.

TOMATITO

The Gypsy influence on flamenco is one of the art form's most important ingredients. The playful fieriness and 'otherness' of the music can almost certainly be traced to this well-established yet often marginalised group in Spanish society. Musicologists may find elements from Byzantine, Moorish and other Mediterranean styles in the general flamenco mix, yet it is the unique Gypsy spark that makes it one of the world's most important musical legacies. Underlying this is the fact that a large percentage of the great flamenco singers have hailed from Gypsy backgrounds, as have many dancers. Among guitarists the group has generally been less well represented. The most celebrated exception to this trend, however, is the Almería-born genius José Fernández Torres, better known by his *apodo* Tomatito ('little tomato').

As is so often the case with flamenco greats, Tomatito grew up in a flamenco family. His father and grandfather were both guitarists who went under the name 'Tomate' (despite being in a desert, Almería is a horticultural centre known for its tomatoes). Young José grew up playing the guitar and made his debut as a soloist at the local *peña*, or flamenco club, at the age of ten.

The family soon moved to Málaga, a city with a stronger flamenco tradition, which is where Tomatito's career began to take off. It was here, when still a youngster, that he first met the mythical (and fellow

Gypsy) singer Camarón de la Isla. In his early work, Camarón had been accompanied by Paco de Lucía, but after a fierce argument in a New York hotel room (the details of which are unknown), the two artists went their separate ways. Tomatito quickly filled the gap left in de Lucía's wake, and Camarón and Tomatito went on to form one of the most powerful and artistically successful partnerships in the history of flamenco – one that lasted until the singer's death in 1991.

'Camarón gave me everything I have,' Tomatito later said. 'He made me.'

The spectacular alchemy between the two men is still evident from their first recordings together, notably on the 1979 album *La Leyenda del Tiempo*, one of the most ground-breaking records in the art form. They combine effortlessly and flawlessly as though made for each other: Tomatito's guitar produces a perfect platform and counterpoint for Camarón's extraordinary and unequalled voice. Look out for video footage of the two men performing live, and the connection between them becomes even more evident. For me, one of the most powerful visual images that exists in flamenco is the expression on Tomatito's face as he accompanies Camarón: those eyes speak of admiration, absolute artistic union with his partner, and what can only be described as love.

Camarón's untimely death at the age of only forty-one was a low point for the world of flamenco, but painfully so for Tomatito.

'I went through a bad time,' he says. 'Everything was broken for me. I still haven't heard anyone sing like him.'

Many feared that the experience might end his career, yet, amazingly, he came back, reinventing himself as a solo performer who went on to become one of the most important guitarists of the modern age.

'To play the guitar you have to be in love with the instrument until you die,' he insists. In the two and a half decades since Camarón's death, he has barely stopped, recording some eight albums, writing music for film, collaborating with an impressive number of artists including Frank Sinatra, Elton John, Neneh Cherry, John McLaughlin and Chick Corea, and winning a seemingly endless number of awards, including two Latin Grammys.

Like many in contemporary flamenco, Tomatito has explored other musical forms, bringing in influences from jazz and pop, yet he is perhaps the figure who has strayed the least in these directions, retaining a sound deeply rooted in his flamenco – and Gypsy – upbringing. The spectrum of tone in his playing is vast and versatile, ranging from muscular and rhythmical, to whimsical, impish and heart-wrenchingly delicate, like a reed bending in the breeze, never breaking nor losing sight of where it belongs.

If you are already familiar with his music, you will know what I mean. If his name is new to you, I suggest you start with his first solo album, *Rosas del Amor* and slowly work your way through. It will be a magical, unforgettable ride.

FLAMENCO WEDDINGS

FLAMENCO WEDDING I
NINETEENTH CENTURY

The following is an extract taken from George Borrow's The Zincali, *published in 1841*

Throughout the day there was nothing going on but singing, drinking, feasting and dancing; but the most singular part of the festival was reserved for the dark night. Nearly a ton weight of sweetmeats had been prepared, at an enormous expense, not for the gratification of the palate, but for a purpose purely Gypsy. These sweetmeats of all kinds, and of all forms, but principally yemas, or yolks of eggs prepared with a crust of sugar (a delicious bonnebouche), were strewn on the floor of a large room, at least to the depth of three inches. Into this room, at a given signal, tripped the bride and bridegroom dancing *Romalis*, followed amain by all the Gitanos and Gitanas, dancing *Romalis*. To convey a slight idea of the scene is almost beyond the power of words. In a few minutes the sweetmeats were reduced to a powder, or rather to a mud, the dancers were soiled to the knees with sugar, fruits, and yolks of eggs. Still more terrific became the lunatic merriment. The men sprang high into the air, neighed, brayed, and crowed; whilst the Gitanas snapped their fingers in their own fashion, louder than castanets, distorting their forms into all kinds of obscene attitudes, and uttering words to repeat which were an abomination. In a corner of the apartment capered the while Sebastianillo, a convict Gypsy from Melilla, strumming the guitar most furiously, and producing demoniacal sounds which had some resemblance to Malbrun (Malbrouk), and, as he strummed, repeating at intervals the Gypsy modification of the song:

>   *Chala Malbrun chinguerar,*
>   *Birandon, birandon, birandera –*
>   *Chala Malbrun chinguerar,*
>   *No se bus trutera –*
>   *No se bus trutera.*
>   *No se bus trutera.*
>   *La romi que le camela,*
>   *Birandon, birandon,* etc.

The festival endures three days, at the end of which the greatest part of the property of the bridegroom, even if he were previously in easy circumstances, has been wasted in this strange kind of riot and dissipation. Paco, the Gypsy of Badajoz, attributed his ruin to the extravagance of his marriage festival; and many other Gitanos have confessed the same thing of themselves. They said that throughout the three days they appeared to be under the influence of infatuation, having no other wish or thought but to make away with their substance; some have gone so far as to cast money by handfuls into the street. Throughout the three days all the doors are kept open, and all corners, whether Gypsies or *Busne*, welcomed with a hospitality which knows no bounds.

FLAMENCO WEDDING II
TWENTIETH CENTURY

'There it is.' We had reached the top of a hill and descended to a modern, square-blocked village.

'Whose wedding is this, anyway?' I asked.

'I told you already.'

I was sure she hadn't mentioned a thing.

She parked at the top of a steep hill near an isolated church. Scores of cars were parked chaotically, half blocking the roads, sticking out awkwardly at right-angles, taking up the space of two, or three other vehicles. There was a familiar feel to it. I caught a glimpse of some of the number plates: Málaga, Seville, Cádiz, Madrid, Barcelona. Whoever was getting married had friends from all over the country.

We walked up to the church. People were standing outside the entrance, some passing through to get inside, others milling about chatting. There was a formality and sense of chaos about them that I recognised. Gypsies. I felt a rush of joy. A Gypsy wedding! And it was suddenly comforting to be back amongst them. After months in Granada, away from Madrid, mourning the loss of my friend. This was where I wanted to be.

We joined the crowd, greeted by a few suspicious looks. As two blonds we stood out. But the bride – no more than seventeen – quickly appeared, draped in white chiffon, clinging to her father's arm. She lowered her head modestly and the crowd gathered round her like bees, while her father grinned, his gold teeth shining from behind thin, cracked lips and a weather-worn face. From his waistcoat hung a gold watch chain, while more gold adorned his wrists. On his forearm read a primitive-looking tattoo: *Nací para sufrir* – Born to suffer.

Father and daughter pushed their way through, stopping to talk briefly with uncles, cousins, grandmothers and nephews. Everyone shouted and sang at once on a great wave of energy and enthusiasm. I looked for Grace – we had been separated in the scrum. She was near the bride, talking to a Gypsy man treating her as an important guest, leaning his face towards hers to hear what she was saying above the spiralling din. She smiled and turned away, clapping her hands with the rhythm now pulsating around the bride and her father as they slowly edged their way towards the church doors.

The little building was overflowing, people cramming in around the door, jumping up and down to see above the other heads in front. Grace had disappeared again. I copied some of the young boys and climbed up the pillars in the doorway, hanging on with one hand and leaning out over the crowd to catch a glimpse of the altar. Grace was at the front, being given one of the best positions by the father of the groom. Both mothers were standing on either side, waiting for the ceremony to finish. But the singing started before they had even got half-way through. It was only a religious formality anyway.

The priest braved on, straining to make his voice heard. Meanwhile the congregation shouted, slapped one other on the back, and swapped stories. The guitars began playing *alboreás* – the special Gypsy wedding *palo* – the clapping began, and the whole church exploded into an impromptu flamenco concert. The poor priest began to look disturbed, sweating heavily, blood pressure rising dangerously under the strain of his collar and heavy robes as the cries of *Olé! Olé! Olé!* drowned him out. But moments later the ceremony had ended, the couple left under a hail of rice, and a white dove was released into the air. It flew frantically up above the trees to get away from the madness.

'For her purity,' one of the boys said, pointing up at the bird and grinning. Virginity was all important.

The mass headed down the hill into the village, where a local restaurant was waiting with cold prawns in mayonnaise and *jamón serrano*. The patio had been covered over with white cloth, and long tables laden with wine, beer and bread waited underneath. Everyone made straight for the drinks before sitting down on benches to nibble at the food, shouting and singing. There was no seating plan as far as I could tell, but the natural Gypsy hierarchy asserted itself. The families of the couple, the elders, the strongmen – they could all be made out by the way the others behaved towards them. It was there in the posture, the tilt of the head, the shape of the shoulders.

But as I listened to the violent din of voices all talking at once, I noticed people were beginning to scream: the women first, then the men. We all turned to see what was going on. Some at the back stood up on the tables to get a better look and the young boys rushed forward. An escaped goat was standing by the main table, baying loudly and chewing the tablecloth. The bride screamed and threw herself into the arms of her husband. But he was as frightened as she was. For a moment everyone was still, before the goat, tiring of the tablecloth and doubtless noticing the huge amount of food on the tables, jumped up and started tucking into the three-tiered wedding cake. Everyone fell back in shock, and when one of the braver types tried to shoo it away, he was met a back kick from the animal's powerful hind legs.

'Fetch a stick!' came the cry. The restaurant owner came out from the kitchen with a broom.

'A broom! A broom! Come on Pepe. Charge!' The cries of encouragement came from all sides. The small, overweight man stood at the side, nostrils flaring, the broom in both hands like a Roman infantryman, pointing it at the goat; the goat that was quickly ruining the biggest event in the village all year. He thrust his weapon tentatively, but to little effect. The animal was moving on from the cake to the ham and prawns.

'*Venga, Pepe!*'

The bride was beginning to cry. The restaurant owner gathered himself, then with a shout dropped the broom, ran at the beast and with a great swing slapped it as hard as he could on the head. The goat stumbled sideways, gave a startled yelp and leapt nimbly from the table and on to the ground. With a couple of bounds he was out of the restaurant and running indignantly down the hill, shaking the remaining crumbs of food from his beard. Pepe, however, was not so nimble, and before he could stop himself he had landed where the goat had leapt off, face down in the garlic mushrooms. Everyone was too shocked to say anything for a moment. Then a cry of *Olé! Pepe!* rang out from the back, and the poor man, realising it was his moment, stood up to take a bow before the cheering crowd.

'Drinks are free!' he spluttered above the cries of congratulation, and with the grin of the all-conquering warrior he headed back into the kitchen.

'What about the other one?' the girl next to me said under her breath as we all sat down again. 'There's more than one with horns at that table.'

Her friend sucked her teeth and one of the women started handing out food noisily trying to drown out talk of the bride's alleged infidelity.

A queue was forming: the couple were sitting on a dais, like kings, and each person was passing by, congratulating them and handing over amounts of money. Grace and I joined the back of the line.

'Great day!' I said to the groom as we reached him, and I looked in the direction of his new wife. He looked solemn for minute, then laughed.

'*A que sí!*. Too right!'

The money-giving ceremony lasted an hour and a half. Everyone wanted to make sure their contribution was the one the couple would remember. And with the cash came promises of favours, best wishes for their future children, gifts, embraces, anecdotes, offers of work. When it was all over, the bride was led away by an elderly woman I had noticed earlier. There was something striking about her, an air of importance, accentuated by the vast number of gold and beaded necklaces resting on her chest. But she had remained in the background and didn't seem to be a member of either of the families.

'That woman there,' Grace said. 'That woman is brought here especially to examine the purity of the bride. They call her an *ajuntaora.*'

The bride looked ill, and was quickly led out of sight into a private room. A few glances were exchanged and everything continued as normal.

Barely five minutes had passed, though, when a woman on the other side of the table began tutting.

'Shouldn't take this long,' she said. Her neighbours agreed.

'They'd be out by now.'

'Never takes this long.'

The women looked concerned. The men, serious.

The anxiousness appeared to have reached the main table, where the groom was sitting, pale-lipped, eyes tight like a fist. The bride's family were beginning to flap like birds.

'Too long, too long, now. I always said it.'

Someone was sent out to find out what was going on. The groom stood up sharply, chair flying out from beneath his legs. His brother ran round and grabbed him by the shoulders.

'Wait!' he shouted. 'Wait!'

But the bride's family were also beginning to stand up, arms hanging by their sides, breathing quickly. Then that smell. I recognised it from the bullfight. The portentous smell of blood, the smell that tells you it will be spilled here, soon.

We were all on our feet, the pitch of voices rising higher and higher. The bride's father was trying to calm things down. He smiled and made steadying gestures with his hands, but sweat dripped from his temples, and his hands were shaking. Just now, I thought, the flick of a knife and all is lost. Something had to be done, but I felt a hand on my arm pressing down. I looked and saw the thick silver ring on Grace's finger. Don't do anything, it said. Just watch, observe.

At that moment the old woman came running out of the restaurant clutching a white handkerchief and raised it high for everyone to see, screaming at the top of her lungs. We leant forward: the cloth was embroidered with a red rose in each corner and in the middle there was a dark yellowy stain. The groom's family stared hard for a second, and then an almighty cheer went up, more out of relief than joy. The two fathers embraced each other like brothers and people sat back into their seats with smiles and grins replacing the angry scowls of a moment earlier. The bride was brought forward looking paler than when she had gone inside, and was swamped with well-wishers, lifting her up in the air and dancing with her, parading triumphantly out into the street. Car horns sounded, the men threw off their jackets, tearing at their shirts in ecstasy, until they stood naked from the waist up, waving their arms and shouting like lunatics.

The music started: two guitarists beating out more *alboreás*. The women took turns to dance in a frenzy, some in pairs, each trying to outdo the other.

I began clapping to the rhythm, letting myself feel, once more, taken away by the joy, the all-embracing energy of a flamenco *juerga*. My face flushed and an uncontrollable smile forced itself onto my mouth. Standing there, tapping my foot, letting myself get drunk on it all, as though in a trance. I was aware of a space next to me, though. I turned. Grace had gone. I expected she had found herself another companion. But I spun round the other way and looked up. She was standing outside on a slope by the road on her own, her head clearly visible above the others, looking me directly in the eye.

'Too noisy in there for you?' I asked as I walked up to her.

'I have to go back to Granada. You can stay if you want.'

From Duende: A Journey in Search of Flamenco

FLAMENCO AND SUFISM

FLAMENCO AND SUFISM

In his groundbreaking book *The Sufis* (1964), the writer Idries Shah mentions several Western cultural phenomena which were influenced or inspired by the mystical current of Islam. They include such diverse things as the Troubadour movement, the figure of the Jester, the writings of Cervantes and Goethe (amongst others) and the development of the Tarot. There is also, in Shah's view, a clear relationship between Sufism and flamenco.

That an Eastern tradition might have any impact at all on the folk music of southern Spain would appear curious were it not for the fact that for eight centuries Iberia was the western extreme of the Islamic Empire. The etymology of 'Andalusia' lies in the Arabic name for the peninsula, *Al-Andalus*. Spain was conquered for Islam in 711, at about the same time that Sindh – roughly today's Pakistan – was also coming under Muslim rule. Communications within the Islamic Empire were relatively quick and easy: in the space of a few generations, what had been Visigothic *Hispania* became an integral part of a cultural environment stretching as far east as the Indies.

And the impact of the Islamic world on Spain – and the rest of Europe – was vast. The Alhambra at Granada and the Great Mosque at Córdoba are merely the more visible and obvious manifestations of this heritage. Everything from food to language, art, literature, religion, science, medicine and philosophy were all influenced by centuries-long exposure to Islam.

So what does this have to do with flamenco? Spanish folk music as a whole was hugely influenced by the sounds brought from across the Strait of Gibraltar. You only have to listen to an Aragonese *jota* or an *albá* from the Valencia area and the similarity to a muezzin's chant is immediate and powerful. And flamenco is no less an example. For instance, common 'nonsense' words used in the *cante* include *Lelelelele*, or *Lailo lailo*. These are a garbled form of the Islamic creed *La ilaha illa Allah* ('No god but Allah'). And anyone familiar with Moroccan and North African music will have heard a common rhythm which is the same as a flamenco *tanguillo*. In fact, the great flamenco singer El Lebrijano often performed with Moroccan musicians, insisting that flamenco and the music of North Africa were essentially the same.

So much for an Islamic influence on flamenco, but what about Sufism specifically? Idries Shah was not the only one to spot the connection. In the 1930s a student from Pakistan named Aziz Balouch travelled to Spain, and as soon as he heard flamenco he recognised it as identical to the Sufi music that he played and sang at home. Indeed, the very next night he sang the same songs back to the original performer – none other than Pepe Marchena – only this time in Urdu. Marchena and his guitarist Ramón Montoya were gobsmacked by the foreigner who had just arrived in Andalusia and yet could sing perfect *cante jondo* as though he had been born and raised in a Spanish village. On the spot, Marchena took the young man on as his fellow performer, and Balouch would go on to record under the name *Marchenita* – 'little Marchena'.

In time, Balouch would write about flamenco and his experiences in *Cante jondo – su orígen y evolución*, published in Madrid in 1955. In it he set out his ideas, drawing up a family tree in which he demonstrated the link between Sufi music and flamenco. He described vocal exercises and even a way of life that he saw as ideal for producing the flamenco 'deep song'. His views on sexual abstinence and alcohol, however, did not sit well within the hedonistic flamenco environment of the day, and the book fell – perhaps not surprisingly – somewhat short of being a best-seller.

There are plenty of reasons, however, for believing that both

Balouch and Shah were correct in pointing out the Sufi-flamenco connection. When your correspondent's book on flamenco (*Duende*) first appeared, many readers wrote that they had experienced something very similar to *duende* when listening to music from the Islamic mystical tradition – an altered state known in Arabic and Persian as *hal* (literally 'state'). The sense of other-worldliness that the best flamenco can produce hints in itself at origins within some kind of metaphysical framework. The Gypsy connection between the Indian sub-continent and Spain is also reason to give credence to the link that Balouch was proposing. And then there is the word '*duende*' itself. Spanish etymologists insist it comes from *dueño de casa* – the 'master of the house' – a reference to the invisible spirits who were meant to inhabit a home. But many Spanish intellectuals have a bias in favour of Latin-based origins over Arabic-based ones; it is just as likely that the Arabic word for 'spirit' – *jinn* – is the root. According to the *Quran*, these beings created of 'smokeless fire' not only exist but can have a powerful influence on human lives, appearing without warning and effecting change on our destiny.

What better description of *duende* itself?

This article first appeared in Classical Guitar Magazine *in the autumn of 2017*

INTERVIEW IV

WITH A BRAZILIAN NEWSPAPER

INTERVIEW WITH A BRAZILIAN NEWSPAPER

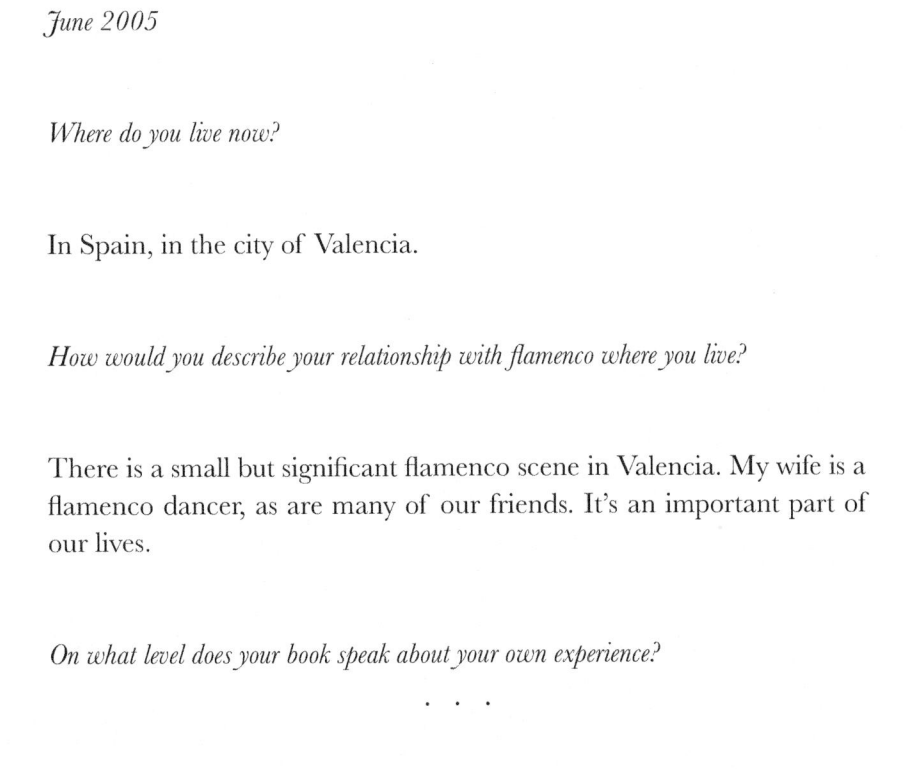

June 2005

Where do you live now?

In Spain, in the city of Valencia.

How would you describe your relationship with flamenco where you live?

There is a small but significant flamenco scene in Valencia. My wife is a flamenco dancer, as are many of our friends. It's an important part of our lives.

On what level does your book speak about your own experience?

. . .

The book is based on experiences I had here in Spain several years ago. It's essentially describing a rite of passage, the process of trying to mature emotionally after years of school and university, where the stress was always on intellectual training. When I'd finished my degree I felt very unformed in many ways, as though there were still so many things to learn before I could call myself an adult. Coming to Spain and learning flamenco were all part of that learning experience. Spain is a very emotional country, very passionate, so it was here that certain parts of me were woken for the first time.

How do you see the flamenco dance and music current background in Spain and around the world? Does it update itself, keep itself traditional...

There is a constant process of renewal in flamenco – and a constant counter-current of people trying to keep it the same and stop it from changing. This tug-of-war is perhaps how it should be: some artists experiment so much within flamenco that you feel something of its essence gets lost. On the other hand, it cannot remain a 'museum piece', as the Granada singer Enrique Morente insists. It needs to move in order to stay alive, otherwise it can become stagnant. But it's always a case of trying to evolve while remaining true to its roots. In the end it depends on individual taste. *Flamencos* can spend hours arguing over what is and what isn't flamenco.

In your opinion, is there any demystification of the genre after the first contacts, or the opposite happens, I mean, the mythical element gets even stronger?

It comes and goes. Perhaps you lose some of the romantic notions you had before, and about the people involved, and I have become disenchanted with flamenco at times. But then something will always happen to make you fall in love with it again, usually when you're least expecting it: hearing a Gypsy singing as he passes under your window in the street, for example. That's when I feel the 'magic' of flamenco most strongly – if you try to grab hold of it, it will fly away; but if you let it come to you, it will find you.

Which is the biggest challenge that flamenco imposes on you as a musician?

Probably the rhythm – it's absolutely essential. Right-hand technique on the guitar is where you start and you have to master it completely before you can go on to anything else.

... and as a member of the audience?

Flamenco shouldn't necessarily be a challenge for the audience. I've been at concerts with some people who get all worried about 'not appreciating' the music or the dance properly. But if it touches you and you enjoy it, that is the only important thing. As you learn more about it, you can appreciate the subtleties more, but if flamenco is for you, you will know, whether you've learnt it or not.

...and as a human being?

People need to find their own flamenco and decide what it means to them. There are plenty out there who will try to tell you that 'flamenco is this' or 'flamenco is that', and get quite angry if you have a different opinion. I don't think any one view of flamenco should ever be imposed on anyone else.

Who are the best singer and the best dancer in your opinion? Why?

. . .

Enrique Morente is my favourite singer, precisely because I feel he gets the balance between tradition and innovation about right. He has an encyclopaedic knowledge of the *cante*, but isn't afraid to try new things and push it in new directions. The best dancer at the moment, also from Granada, is Eva Yerbabuena, an incredibly moving performer who is the only dancer who has moved me to tears.

During your book, we follow your learning process as flamenco, as a journalist and also as a writer... How did you discover yourself as a writer?

I had some friends who were also writers who encouraged me. As the book progressed they were able to give me excellent advice and were very patient with me. I was very lucky in that regard.

Which is the toughest challenge to write about this issue?

Trying to put into words the power of the music and the effect it had on me and people around me. You're having to translate one art form into another. It would be like trying to paint a novel.

Did you look for a definite artistic style also during the writing process?

No. There probably were influences on me, but they were mostly subconscious. I thought it important to try and find a personal 'voice' early on in my career. Although whether or not I have succeeded, I can't say.

The story of a foreign man who arrives in Spain to learn about flamenco and ends falling in love with a dancer doesn't sound like a cliché to you?

. . .

I'll tell my wife. Although I'm not sure if she'd appreciate our relationship being described as a 'cliché'. People from northern countries have long been coming to the south in search of 'passion'. For many, Spain and Latin countries are simply sexier than back home. There's a long literary tradition of this, from E M Forster to Ernest Hemingway. It may all sound a bit too familiar, but thousands have gone through similar experiences and never written about it: it's just part of the dynamic and relationship between north and south.

Finally, can you describe 'duende'?

I didn't give a definition in the book precisely because I don't think it's something that can be pinned down. It has to be felt, and different people will feel different things. If you 'define' it, you lose it.

INFLUENCES

INFLUENCES

Zine insisted on coming with me to the flamenco *tablao* that night. He wanted to see something of the city – *Ishbiliya*, the Moors had called it, and he referred to it by the old Arabic name. On the way, brightly lit above the orange trees and shiny black carriages ferrying tourists, we passed the *Giralda* – the former minaret of the main mosque, now the bell tower of the cathedral.

Across the square stood the Alcázar: Seville's Alhambra, a lusciously decorated Moorish-style palace still used as a royal residence. Its delicate archways, pools of water and *yeso* plastered ceilings had been built for a Christian king, Pedro the Cruel; the royal escutcheon painted on the walls of his bedchamber proclaimed in Arabic script: 'Glory to our Sultan Don Pedro, May Allah Aid and Protect Him.'

At the *tablao*, Zine pushed his way towards the front to grab us a seat. Then Amadeo showed up; he was an old *flamenco* friend who I hadn't seen for years. The three of us managed to sit at the end of one of the refectory tables that stretched the length of the hall. *La Carbonería* was among the few places where you didn't have to pay to watch live performances.

Amadeo and I quickly caught up on each other's news. Seeing him now would be a great opportunity for my search. I knew he was interested in the history of flamenco and Spanish folk music. 'Talking to Amadeo's like talking to a book,' others often said of him. Perhaps he could help me understand the Moorish influence on the art form.

Seville had been the musical centre of Spain for hundreds of years. Court composition had flourished in Córdoba, the capital of caliphal Al-Andalus, but when this started to mix with popular styles, Seville's musical importance grew.

'When a wise man dies in Seville,' the twelfth-century polymath Averroes had said, 'they take his books to be sold in Córdoba. And when a musician dies in Córdoba they take his instruments to be sold in Seville.'

This proud, floral city, with its perfume of orange blossom and its vibrant colours, seemed to live off music. A whole folk dance – *Sevillanas* – had been named after it, and numerous flamenco songs made reference to the Triana district on the east bank of the Guadalquivir.

> *El río Guadalquivir se quejaba una mañana:*
> *'Tengo que elegir entre Sevilla y Triana, y no sé cómo*
>   *elegir.*
> *'¡Ay! ¿Quién pudiera fundir en un perfume menta y*
>   *canela?'*

> The Guadalquivir cried one morning:
> 'I have to choose between Seville and Triana but
>   don't know how.
> 'Who could make perfume by mixing mint and
>   cinnamon?'

For centuries Triana, a run-down area, like a muddy reflection of the imperial city on the opposite bank, had been home to Gypsies and workers, whose lasting legacy came from their music and dancing. It was not a romantic place: in fact some guide books warned you not to go there, or if you did, at least to keep a tight grip on handbags and wallets. A few bars on the river bank were cashing in on its reputation as a flamenco heartland.

Despite having been involved in flamenco and having a fascination for Moorish Spain, I'd never successfully joined up these two interests. I knew about the theories that the word 'flamenco' itself came from the Arabic *felah manju*, or 'escaped peasant', and that *olé* was in fact a borrowing from the Arabic phrase *wallahi*. But apart from that I still wasn't clear what the Moorish influence on flamenco had really been.

'No-one can say for sure: that's the problem,' Amadeo told me. 'Flamenco's an oral art form, so there aren't many written records to give us clues. Then it's a mixture of Gypsy stuff, Andalusian folk music and some Moorish stuff as well. It's almost impossible to separate all the different strands. *¿Me explico?* Understand?'

Amadeo was the best kind of *flamenco* in my mind: a Bohemian who had seen some of the harsher sides of life, but who had come out smiling on the other side. He had a heavily lined face, dark rings under his eyes and a volcanic voice, but a light shone from him, like someone who had not only lived, but learnt. I knew that for years he'd kept himself alive busking around Europe, on the underground or in the street, with the odd gig here and there at a bar or pub: a kind of flamenco troubadour, picking up bits and pieces of musical knowledge as he wandered the world. His style of playing was a bit old-fashioned for some, but his sense of rhythm was perfect.

'Islamic music has modes, like the different *palos* in flamenco,' he went on. 'They call them *maqamat*, or *tubu'* in Morocco. Each one with its own distinctive key and beat. You know, like *bulerías* or *alegrías* for us. I've heard Mauritanian musicians playing the same rhythms as a *petenera*.'

We both touched the wooden bench beneath us to ward off the evil eye as he mentioned the secret *palo*. Similar in structure to a *soleá* or a *bulería* – yet with one important difference – it was thought by Gypsies to have some magical protection about it, so that for years no one recorded it or taught it outside a select group. Even mentioning its name, like now, brought out the superstitious in many.

'I think maybe that's why we think of it as the "mother *palo*",' Amadeo said. 'Any twelve-beat flamenco rhythm finds its origins in it, and it probably comes from Africa or the Middle East, but no one is allowed to talk about it. *¿Me explico?* It's taboo.'

I nodded. Across from our table, a pair of Gypsies were sitting at the edge of the stage, a young man with long hair hunched over his cigarette, and next to him a man of about fifty, dressed in a grey suit with white shirt and crimson cravat, a gold chain hanging loosely from his wrist, and grey boots of soft leather, his hand resting on an ebony cane. Proud and composed, he looked at me for a minute and smiled like a cat.

'What about the Gypsy influence, then?' I asked, turning back to Amadeo.

'This is exactly what I mean about the *petenera*,' he said. We both touched wood again. It felt almost blasphemous mentioning the word twice in quick succession.

'The Gypsies were responsible for the change in the *palo*,' Amadeo said. 'The shift of the first beat from the 'one' back to the 'twelve'. That's how we get *soleares* and other *palos* from it. That's their genius. Simple, but it changes the entire *feeling* of the music.'

'OK,' I said, trying to get back to our original theme, 'apart from, er, that *palo*, are there any other obvious Moorish influences in flamenco?'

'In Yemen I often heard *tanguillos*,' he said. And with his tongue he began clicking the gallop-like rhythm of the flamenco song, marking the beat with his finger like a conductor. 'Then there's our instruments.' He began a list on his fingers, ticking each item off with his claw-like right hand, each nail a perfectly filed lump of flesh hardened and protected for playing. 'Drums, trumpets, hornpipes and rebecs, the precursor of the viol family, all come from the Middle East. Tambourine? *Pandereta* comes from the Arabic *bandair*. The guitar? Comes from the Arabic lute according to some. Can't have flamenco without the guitar. And that's largely Ziryab's influence. See what I mean?'

Ziryab, the man who in the ninth century introduced everything from toothpaste to chess to Europe, had long fascinated me. A musician of exceptional ability, his jealous teacher had him banished from the imperial court in Baghdad when the young apprentice revealed the full extent of his talents at a concert before the Caliph. Soon afterwards, Ziryab ended up in Al-Andalus, a distant and politically independent outpost of the Muslim world, till then effectively cut off from the cultural flowering that was taking place in the Islamic heartlands. Settling in Córdoba as the emir's court musician, he introduced the backwater *Andalusis* to the latest fashions from what was then the Paris or New York of its day: seasonal colours for clothes (dark in winter, white in summer); short hair cuts for both men and women – veils and turbans didn't become the norm until much later on; table etiquette; home furnishings; and of course, the latest tastes in music. This Beau Brummell of Al-Andalus, as he had often been described, also revolutionised the lute, effecting a major step into its development into the guitar by adding a fifth string. The original four had represented the classical humours; what was missing, according to Ziryab, was the 'heart'. Over a thousand years later Paco de Lucía had named one his records after this ancient style guru in recognition of the debt flamenco owed him.

And then there were *saetas*.

'Ah, now that really is an Arabic thing, *pues*,' Amadeo said when I mentioned them.

These were haunting chants sung in honour of the Virgin Mary or Jesus during the Easter Week parades. Their strange, twisting melodies with sliding quarter tones sounded very like muezzin calls to prayer.

> *Y las golondrinas quitaron*
> *las espinas a Jesús*
> *y no pudieron desclavarlo*
> *con sus picos de la cruz.*

The swallows picked
the needles from Jesus' hair,
but with their beaks were unable
to bring him down from the cross.

During the singing, waves of woe rose among the public in mass displays of grief. They reminded me of the annual Shi'i Ashura festivals in Iran and Iraq. Shi'ism, an early break-away branch of Islam, had never taken root in Al-Andalus, which remained decidedly orthodox, or Sunni, throughout its history. Yet the similarities between Holy Week and Ashura were striking: the death of a holy man – Imam Hussein, in the case of the Shi'is – was marked by large processions, public weeping and self-flagellation. Another Muslim echo in the Spanish Easter festivities was the organisation of the participants into brotherhoods, or *hermandades*. These cloaked figures with pointed hoods that masked their faces – the inspiration for the uniform of the Ku Klux Klan – originated in semi-secret religious societies in Al-Andalus: they still existed in Morocco and were involved in processions on feast days to local holy sites.

'Saetas,' Amadeo shouted in my ear as I strained to hear him above the sound of the new flamenco *cantaor* starting his set, 'comes from the Arabic word *ghaita*. They used to sing them in the evenings to entertain the kings and caliphs. You can still hear them sung in some parts of Algeria. And they still call them *ghaitas*.'

I smiled as I turned back to look at the performance on stage. The singer was slumped in his chair, the usual round-shouldered posture to achieve the right resonance in the thorax; dark skin, hair glistening under the spots from the wet-look gel he'd applied before coming on.

'The Church, of course, knew about all this Moorish and Gypsy influence on music. That's why they banned certain scales. The flamenco scale – the one we use, right? – that was banned by the Inquisition. They said it was the work of the Devil. Ha! Just because we jump three semitones. *¿Me explico?* Can't do that, they said…'

From Andalus: Unlocking the Secrets of Moorish Spain

MUSIC FATIGUE

MUSIC FATIGUE

For two years I had done little but listen to music, think about music, play music. There was so much music I barely spent a moment without some tune, some rhythm playing itself out in my mind. First thing in the morning, as I was having a shower, over lunch, walking in the park. And when I tried to go to sleep. This was the worst. There were times when I would spend hours trying in vain to switch my head off, fingers on my left hand involuntarily twitching as an idea for a *falseta* or a variation on a *compás* would play itself over and over again. And I would be amazed at how brilliant my ideas were as the new sound appeared to compose itself in front of me. I must be a genius, I would tell myself. If only I could plug some software into my brain and download all this for later.

But the next day would come and the wonderful music that had kept me awake only a few hours beforehand would vanish and leave me empty-handed, my genius seriously undermined. So I tried getting up once or twice to try out the ideas on the guitar. Bad move. The intricate melodies that had been so clear and easy when in my head became discordant twangings that sounded nothing like what I had meant to play. I persevered for a while, convinced that eventually the effort would pay off and the world would benefit from my musical achievements. But after half a dozen sleepless nights with no flamenco symphony under my belt, I had to conclude I was no new Mozart, and that I would probably be better off sleeping during those hours.

I began to listen to less music in general. Whereas before I would always have it playing – a cassette player or a walkman, or just the radio – now I began to crave silence. Just the thought of hearing music would make me feel nauseous, like being offered a rich creamy pudding at the end of an already heavy meal. I had overdosed, was suffering from music fatigue, and wanted nothing more than to hear the natural sounds around me with no artistic interference.

Music, I realised, not only brought joy, but could also – in large doses – become poison.

Y DESPUÉS

Y DESPUÉS

By Federico García Lorca

    Los labirintos
    que crea el tiempo,
    se desvanecen.

    (Sólo queda
    el desierto.)

    El corazón
    fuente del deseo,
    se desvanece.

    (Sólo queda
    el desierto.)

    La ilusión de la aurora
    y los besos,
    se desvanecen.

Sólo queda
el desierto.
Un ondulado
desierto.

AFTER

The labyrinths
of time
fade away.

(Only the desert
remains.)

The heart,
fountain of desire,
fades away.

(Only the desert
remains.)

The illusion of dawn,
of a kiss,
fades away.

Only the desert
remains.
A rippling
desert.

FINDING OTHER THINGS

FINDING OTHER THINGS

Carmen and I were accompanied by Luis and his kick-boxing girlfriend.

'I wouldn't miss this if I was dead,' he said emphatically as we walked round the back of the Alhambra.

'I tell you, sex on tap is great, but it doesn't beat being able to listen to Paco.'

It seemed things weren't so great with his girlfriend again.

'She just seems to think I'm some sort of punch bag. And I told her: a bit of rough – no problem. But at the right moment. I mean look,' – he showed me the bruises on his arms – 'I can't carry on like this. Martial arts and flamenco, they just don't mix.'

Carmen, meanwhile, was skipping ahead, urging us to hurry up. The news had just come through of her acceptance at the Conservatory.

'All thanks to Juana,' she said. 'I'm finally getting out of this place.'

We found our seats and settled down under the clear night sky. The open auditorium was set in beautiful gardens, with the thick sweet scent of *galán de noche* blowing over our heads like liquor fumes. There was the usual noise and excitement, cigarette smoke and bronzed limbs. But I needed a pee.

'You can't go now! He's about to come on,' Luis cried.

'Back in a tick.'

I made my way out of the auditorium, out on to the gravel path, and looked for the loo. There were people everywhere, long tables serving as makeshift bars, guards and ticket collectors, but I couldn't find the toilet. In the rush I decided there was nothing for it but to go behind a tree. I cut through a gap in the hedges and started heading cross-country. After a few minutes I found what looked to be suitable spot, pulled down my fly and relaxed. No-one would see me there, I was certain. But trying to urinate as fast as I could, I heard a rustle nearby. Someone else had had the same idea. I looked up and saw a man with long dark blond hair, a long mournful face and an equally astonished expression as my own. It was Paco.

'*Hombre, Paco!*' I said. Here I was, in the Generalife, pissing next to the greatest guitarist of all time.

'*Hola*,' he said nervously.

'No toilets backstage?'

'This is backstage.'

I felt a complete fool.

'Oh. Sorry. It's just I couldn't find…'

'Don't worry. Neither could I. Everyone gets nervous just before going on, and all the toilets were taken. I couldn't wait.'

We both finished at the same time and zipped ourselves up.

'Nice meeting you,' I said.

'And you.' he smiled, turning to leave.

'Good luck tonight.'

'Thanks for coming.' And he shook my hand.

I watched as he walked away. He seemed uncomfortable on his feet. Too much sitting down practicing, probably. Then I looked down at my hand. This was one handshake that would definitely be washed away.

I was back in my seat just as Paco came on to the stage. He looked different up there, dressed in his traditional white shirt and black waistcoat. The guitar on his lap changed him, somehow. More powerful, more presence.

'You almost missed him,' Carmen hissed.

The concert started with a *taranta*. Paco sat alone on stage, gradually drawing the audience into the concert as they settled down, and the hum of voices in the hot perfumed air of the garden fell silent.

For the following piece more members of the band appeared and the concert moved up a gear.

But something happened when El Grilo – the tall, powerful-looking dancer with greased-back black hair – appeared. Previously playing percussion on the sidelines, he threw himself on to the centre of the stage towards the end of a *bulería* and started dancing, taking us all by surprise. The man was panther-like: commanding and graceful, and with clean, elegant movements he managed to mesmerize the audience. There was absolute joy in the way he danced; unaffected, playful, almost childlike.

The hairs began to lift on the back of my neck and arms, and a circling, electric energy passed through the audience. He had it, he had *duende*: holding us all down in our seats and seizing our attention. And we watched him, his tall, dark animal-like form hammering the floor with immense speed, sweat flying from his head, arms thrust out at his side. A moment of near-madness descending upon us for a second, and then, just as quickly, flying away, leaving a hollow, joyous echo.

His performance inspired the other players. Paco, I could see, had been coasting along until then. But now he had something to play for, to play against, as did the other members of the band, and they all responded with more energy, greater passion. It produced a spark, each one trying to improve on the other, while the audience sat back in enjoyment, music flowing over and into us, like the scent of flowers. Paco's playing was sublime.

'I wonder if I could play like that one day,' I asked myself.

'Twenty years practice, eight hours a day,' said Luis. 'That's what it takes to play like that.'

'You need genius for that,' Carmen added.

'She's right. The girl's right.'

Genius and obsessive discipline. It felt like a tall order. Would I ever be able to produce *duende*?

I was finding other things.

From Duende: A Journey in Search of Flamenco

A FLAMENCO GLOSSARY

A FLAMENCO GLOSSARY

Flamenco has its own vocabulary, one which even ordinary Spaniards – if they have no interest in, or knowledge of, the art form – struggle to understand. So here is a glossary containing the most common terms for which there is no direct translation into English:

Alzapúa – A rapid right-hand guitar technique. Generally there are two variations: in the first the thumb strikes down on one of the bass strings, resting on the string beneath, which it then strikes as well before flicking back upwards on the trebles (although usually avoiding the first string). This creates a playful 1-2-3 rhythm with the emphasis on the 1. The first strike can be doubled to create a 1-2-3-4 rhythm in which the stress would be on the 2 or 3. In the second variation the thumb merely strikes back upwards on the second bass string, avoiding the trebles altogether.

Ayeo – Generally comes at the start of the song (*cante*). A ritual, almost sacred moment when the performer sings *¡Ay!* before the main lyrics begin. Often associated with the *jondo* (*q.v.*) style, it serves many purposes: to fine-tune the singer's voice; to signal that the singing is about to begin; to strike a note of harmony with the other performers; and to create the right atmosphere for the performance.

Compás – The rhythm of a particular piece of flamenco music. There are several, but the most distinctive is one based on twelve beats, with stresses on the 3, 6, 8, 10 and 12, which is heard in *bulerías, soleares, alegrías* and other styles. Given flamenco – and particularly Gypsy – playfulness and love of off-beats, there are a seeming endless number of variations to this basic pattern. Other common *compases* include the 3/4 (*sevillanas* and *fandangos*) and 4/4 (*tangos, rumba*). To be *fuera de compás* (i.e. not in rhythm, not in the groove) is cardinal sin *número uno* for a flamenco performer.

Duende – The ineffable, indefinable power and magic that can come in a flamenco performance, the moment when the hair stands up on the back of your neck and you feel as if you have had a fleeting experience of something far removed from ordinary life. Literally '*duende*' means goblin or earth spirit, which doesn't quite work in English ('Hey man, you've got goblin…'). So it's better to use the original Spanish term.

Escobilla – Literally 'brush' or 'broom', this refers to the section of the dance when the emphasis is on footwork, the guitar usually providing a simple, rhythmic backing while the dancer shows off his or her percussive skills in an increasingly rapid and explosive display.

Falseta – Melodic pieces played by the guitarist (*tocaor*) in-between the series of chords which define a particular flamenco style (*palo, q.v.*). Since the time of the great innovator Ramón Montoya (d. 1949), *falsetas* have grown in importance in parallel with the evolution of the guitarist's role, and today can make up almost the entirety of a soloist's repertoire. When accompanying a singer (*cantaor*) or dancer (*bailaor*), the guitarist will insert *falsetas* during pauses in the artist's performance.

. . .

Jaleo – The various exclamations of appreciation made by members of a flamenco group during a solo section by one of the others – either dancer, singer or guitarist. The best known expression is *Olé* (the emphasis is commonly on the first syllable), which comes from the Arabic *wallahi* ('By God!'). Other expressions include *Arsa*, and *Eso es* ('that's it!').

Jondo – From an Andalusian pronunciation of the Spanish word *hondo* – 'deep'. *Cante jondo* refers to the deepest, darkest and many say most difficult styles within flamenco, namely the *soleá* and *seguiriya*. A kind of snobbery can be found within the flamenco community where only an appreciation of the *jondo* is a sign of being a true aficionado, with a certain sniffiness directed towards fans of the 'lighter' forms such as *tangos* and *bulerías*.

Palmas – The rhythmic clapping which marks the *compás* (*q.v.*) in many flamenco performances. *Palmas* are taken very seriously, with some artists specialising in them. Get them wrong and at best you'll be made very aware of your lowly position in the hierarchy. There are two basic styles: *sonoras*, in which the fingers of one hand strike the palm of the other, creating a clean, sharp sound; and *sordas*, in which the palms of both hands are 'hollowed' and strike together, making a softer sound which doesn't upstage the voice of the *cantaor*, or the *falseta* (*q.v.*) currently being played.

Palo – The word used to describe the different styles or musical structures within flamenco, e.g. *bulerías, tangos, alegrías* etc. Each *palo* has its distinct feeling, deriving from the rhythm, chord structure and kinds of lyrics associated with it. For a guitarist there are, in a manner of speaking, fewer *palos*, as some differ from one another mainly because of changes in the dance or song alone. For example a guitarist's performance of a *cantiña* would be almost identical to an *alegría*.

· · ·

A palo seco – A song performed without any guitar accompaniment. Commonly the *tonás*, and the *martinete*, which is sung with the rhythmic accompaniment of a hammer on an anvil, a reference to the traditional occupation of many Gypsies in the past.

Rasgueado – A guitar-strumming technique particularly associated with flamenco, in which – usually – all the strings are made to vibrate in a rapid movement of the hand, opening the fingers almost like a fan and striking one after the other with the nails. There are variations and a guitarist will often stick with the one that works best for him or her. The *rasgueado* is one of the first and most basic techniques that a would-be *tocaor* (*q.v.*) learns.

Tablao – A flamenco performance venue, often a bar or restaurant. *Tablaos* came into existence in the 1950s, when the Spanish tourist industry began to take off, replacing the *cafés cantantes* of the past. Well known *tablaos* include Casa Patas, Corral de la Morería, Café de Chinitas and Las Carboneras – all in Madrid.

Tocaor – The word generally used to describe a flamenco guitar player. The word *guitarrista* also exists in Spanish, and can be used in a flamenco context. The difference between the two is that a *tocaor* is generally viewed as both a composer as well as a performer.

Zapateado – From *zapato*, meaning 'shoe'. The *zapateado* is an important element of the dance in which the *bailaor* or *bailaora* shows off their footwork skills, creating complex percussive rhythms in a growing crescendo, often producing one of the most emotionally intense moments of the performance. The guitarist will commonly remain silent for most of this section, coming in towards the end as the *palo* (*q.v.*) moves towards its finale.

A SPANISH REVIEW OF DUENDE

LA VANGUARDIA REVIEW OF DUENDE

September 2010

The following review appeared in the Barcelona newspaper La Vanguardia *on the publication of the Spanish edition of* Duende *in 2010. It acts as an interesting counterpoint to the book itself: while* Duende *is partly about an Englishman's observations of Spain, the review in turn reflects certain Spanish ideas about the English. And while it is generally positive, I should point out that in no way do I recognise or identify with the sentiments expressed at the end, which are solely the reviewer's own*

When it comes to obsession, size matters. The object is irrelevant as long as it is a colossal obsession, burning and self-destructive. The more it burns, the better it is to read about it; not so much for the *schadenfreude*, as for our fascination with the fierceness of the passion itself, that frozen and absolute and dominant passion we call obsession.

The protagonist and author of *Duende* is a weak, pallid Englishman called Jason Webster, a typical product of Oxbridge, who goes through life like a distressed tuning fork, saying sorry when you tread on his foot, moving around campus on a bicycle, reading the works of dead poets, and eating crap food. Until one day: a terrible day when his girlfriend leaves him and Jason flips, with the result that he comes to Spain to learn flamenco guitar. What appears to be a typical impulsive act by someone with a broken heart (usually you end up doing something you'll be ashamed of the rest of your life, like shaving your balls or getting a Peter Pan tattoo) in Jason becomes a pure and frightful obsession. *El Guiri* – as everyone ends up calling him – moves first to Alicante and then to Madrid, finally settling in Granada, all the while perfecting his playing of the guitar when not imbibing cognac or snorting white powdery substances.

Webster's tale of his Iberian life is an excellent read, not least because his adventures are legion. He makes a hunter cuckold by sleeping with his flamenco-dancer wife, travels inside the boot of car, hooks up with a group of cocaine-addicted Gypsies (who share their dwelling with a defecating donkey), becomes a street musician, is involved in car crash with a stolen vehicle, and is the involuntary witness of a knife fight, amongst other things. And not once in all of this does he ever say: 'For fuck's sake! Why did I ever leave my quiet life back in Oxford?'

As a book which views traditions and cultures of the country through fresh eyes, certain fragments sound like the kinds of conversation you might have in a lift: the heat in Madrid is dry, the Spanish shout a lot, there is a disgusting thing you put in your mouth called *Ducados* [cigarettes]. My god, they kill bulls here as well, don't they? These phrases spoken by a Spaniard would be the clichés that one might use in conversation with the doorman. In the mouth of a Hispanist who only days before was cycling through the English countryside, they have a revelatory quality about them. And this is another of the charms of *Duende*: how does a recently arrived Englishman see us? I'll tell you, so you don't get any ideas about being European: they see us as half-Arab dwarfs who always make a huge racket, who give scarce attention to personal hygiene, and have no respect for personal space.

Well observed, Jason.

WHAT IS DUENDE?

WHAT IS DUENDE?

In the two and a half years that these articles have been appearing in *Classical Guitar*, one subject has been mentioned in passing on several occasions, but never dealt with specifically. It is, however, essential to any understanding of flamenco – and the whole of flamenco, not just the art of the *tocaor*. Such is its importance that without it one could say there is no flamenco to begin with, and so it needs addressing.

'*Duende*' is a complex and subtle concept, so much so that whole books could be written on it (in fact, your correspondent had a stab at it himself some years back…). Despite lying at the very heart of flamenco, any definition of it can only ever hope to be an approximation, for *duende* has to be experienced to be understood and appreciated. To borrow a definition from Eastern thought: 'He who tastes, knows.'

Look the word up in a dictionary and it will tell you that '*duende*' means 'goblin' or 'earth spirit' in English. That gives us a clue, for the *duende* experience exists outside ordinary reality. In a flamenco context, it encapsulates the moment in a performance when, inexplicably, your hair stands on end, something disturbing and magnificent seems to stir in your blood, and you have the sense of possibility – a whisper, only partially heard – of the existence of worlds beyond worlds.

The feeling may be fleeting, gone almost as soon as it is registered.

Or it may be sustained for a considerable period. But how long it lasts is of relatively small importance for, in essence, it exists outside of time itself, and a single, concentrated point of a *duende* experience may take years to digest, can – and frequently does – cause significant change in people's lives.

Flamenco is not the only vehicle for *duende*: in a Spanish context you may also, on occasion, hear the word used in the world of bullfighting. Yet it is with flamenco that it has become more closely associated; the very strangeness of Andalusian sounds and rhythms hinting at realms of experience which lie beyond ordinary ken. Certain performers have been closely associated with it: the great *cantaor* of the late 20th century Camarón de la Isla was said to have an almost unique ability to produce *duende* at will. This is no idle claim, for the majority of flamenco artists will talk about *duende* as something akin to a gift, a quality which, with a will of its own, can come and go, can bless a performance with its presence just as soon as it vanishes again. All that the musicians and dancers can do is provide a setting, the right circumstances, for it to manifest.

The most powerful *duende* experiences can be had during live flamenco acts, but personally one of my earliest was listening to La Niña de los Peines – a giant of the mid-20th century – singing a *Lorquiana*, a song with lyrics by the Granadan poet Federico García Lorca. I practically wore the vinyl out playing the same track again and again, such was the impact it had on me and the curious, intoxicating nature of the feeling it evoked.

Lorca himself tried to explain *duende* to non-Spanish audiences.

'Everything that has black sounds in it,' he wrote in 1933, 'has *duende*.' And went on to describe how a Gypsy woman he knew had exclaimed on hearing Bach for the first time that the German composer's music also had *duende*.

Lorca was, of course, later murdered outside Granada shortly after the outbreak of the Spanish Civil War in 1936, and has become not only a symbol of the bloody repression that took place at that time, but a revered figure within flamenco. Something of the nature of the man and his work – his brilliance, intuitive power, poetic talent and also his tragic end – carry with them hints of *duende* itself. For *duende* can be as disturbing as it is vivifying, can speak as much of 'distance' as of 'presence'. I have seen men rip their shirts open with near madness and grief because of it, while others sat in total silence, motionless, heads bowed as though in communion.

Duende is one of the most powerful, but also most personal, experiences that anyone can have. Which is why it can never be defined. It can speak of joy, grief, ecstasy, emptiness, solitude, oneness – all manner of feelings, often several at once. Much depends on the vessel into which it is poured.

Its existence, whether perceived or not, goes a long way to explaining the perennial attraction to – and not infrequent rejection of – flamenco within many different people all over the world.

And for a performer – a guitarist, singer or dancer – is there a correct way to approach *duende*? Perhaps by not trying to 'approach' it at all. *Duende* exists, but is rarely spoken about among *flamencos*, viewed as something almost sacred, to be treated with respect.

'You cup your hands,' one elderly *cantaora* once told me. 'If it rains, you may catch water. But only the sky can make it rain.'

Then she jabbed her finger hard into the centre of my chest.

'The question is, if it comes, do you deserve it?'

This article first appeared in Classical Guitar Magazine *in the summer of 2017*

ACKNOWLEDGMENTS

Certain people have become indispensable for the continuation of the *Mosaics of Spain* series, principally Felicity Laughton and Spike Golding. I owe them both a huge debt.

This book, as with all of them, ultimately exists thanks to one person, however: Salud, *que está en cada página*.

ABOUT THE AUTHOR

JASON WEBSTER was born in 1970 and spent his childhood in the US, Britain and Germany. He first moved to Spain in the early 1990s having graduated in Arabic and Islamic History from St John's College, Oxford. His books have sold in over fifteen countries around the world.

In 2011, Webster's short story, 'Rafaelillo' was included in *Ox Travels*, a collection of pieces by twenty-five leading travel writers published in aid of Oxfam with an introduction by Michael Palin. He has presented and appeared in radio and TV documentaries for the BBC, Channel 5 and the Discovery Channel.

Webster is an award-winning photographer, co-founder of the Bridport School of Writing, and from 2014 to 2017 was the flamenco correspondent for *Classical Guitar* magazine. In addition, Webster has written extensively for British and Spanish newspapers, including *The Financial Times*, *The Telegraph*, *The Guardian*, *The Observer*, *The Independent* and *El Asombrario*. He is married to the flamenco dancer Salud and has two children.

If you'd like to subscribe to his **free *Pearls of Spanish Genius*** newsletter, please visit his website, www.jasonwebster.net, where you can also find out more about his books.

    facebook.com/jasonwebsterauthor
    twitter.com/JWebsterwriter
    instagram.com/jasonwebsterwriter

REQUEST

Good reviews are a great help

If you enjoyed this book, please review it on **Amazon**, **Goodreads**, or anywhere else you prefer.

Thank you.

The Corsario team

Printed in Great Britain
by Amazon